WONDERDADS

THE BEST DAD/CHILD ACTIVITIES IN WASHINGTON DC

CONTACT WONDERDADS

WonderDads books may be purchased for educational and promotional use. For information, please email us at store@wonderdads.com.

If you are interested in partnership opportunities with WonderDads, please email us at partner@wonderdads.com.

If you are interested in selling WonderDads books and other products in your region, please email us at hiring@wonderdads.com.

For corrections, recommendations on what to include in future versions of the book, updates or any other information, please email us at info@wonderdads.com.

Book Authored by Caroline Gould & the WonderDads Staff.

Cover & Book Design by Crystal Langley. Proofread by Megan Fearon & the WonderDads Staff.

Activities in this book should only be done with adult supervision. WonderDads encourages parents to not engage in any activities they feel could be harmful to their child or that their child may try to do again without an adult presence. WonderDads assumes no liability for any direct or indirect injuries that occur when using this book.

ISBN: 978-1-935153-56-6

First Printing, 2011

1. 1

WONDERDADS WASHINGTON DC

Table of Contents

pg. 9
The Best of Washington DC

pg. 13
The Best Dad/Child Restaurants

pg. 29
The Best Dad/Child Activities

pg. 53
The Best Dad/Child Stores

pg. 73
The Best Dad/Child Outdoor Parks & Recreation

pg. 89
The Best Dad/Child Unique Adventures

pg. 99
The Best Dad/Child Sporting Events

FREE ACCESS FOR ONE YEAR ON YOUR SMARTPHONE!

Content From this Book, Special Updates & More on your

IPHONE, BLACKBERRY OR ANDROID

Take 10 Seconds to Register at

www.WonderDads.com/mobile.asp

We'll Then Email You the Special Web Address and Your Username/Password

WELCOME TO WONDERDADS WASHINGTON DC

Like so many other Dads, I love being with my kids, but struggle to find the right work/home balance. We are a part of a generation where Dads play much more of an active role with their kids, yet the professional and financial strains are greater than ever. We hope that the ideas in this book make it a little easier to be inspired to do something that makes you a hero in the eyes of your children.

This part of our children's lives goes by too fast, but the memories from a WonderDads inspired trip, event, meal, or activity last a long time (and will probably be laughed about when they grow up). So plan a Daddy day once a week, make breakfast together every Saturday morning, watch your football team every Sunday, or whatever works for you, and be amazed how long they will remember the memories and how good you will feel about yourself in the process.

Our warmest welcome to WonderDads.

Sincerely,

Jonathan Aspatore, **Founder & Dad**
Charlie (4) and Luke (3)

THE TOP TEN OVERALL BEST DAD/CHILD THINGS TO DO

Gravelly Point Park ....pg. 84

Upton Hill Regional Park ....pg. 85

The International Spy Museum ....pg. 36

The Crime and Punishment Museum ....pg. 35

The Smithsonian Air and Space Museum ....pg. 48

Brookside Gardens ....pg. 91

Mount Vernon....................................pg. 95

Glen Echo Park....................................pg. 74

National Building Museum....................................pg. 35

Capitals game at the Verizon Center....................................pg. 100

THE TOP FIVE DAD/CHILD RESTAURANTS

Cereal Bowl....pg. 19
Café Delux....pg. 15
Tacklebox....pg. 23
Johnny Rocket's....pg. 22
Comet Ping Pong....pg. 17

THE TOP FIVE DAD/CHILD ACTIVITIES

The International Spy Museum....pg. 36
The Crime and Punishment Museum....pg. 35
The Smithsonian Air and Space Museum....pg. 48
National Building Museum....pg. 35
The National Zoo....pg. 31

TOP FIVE DAD/CHILD THINGS TO DO ON A RAINY DAY

The International Spy Museum....pg. 36
National Museum of the American Indian....pg. 49
The Smithsonian Natural History Musem....pg. 45
National Building Museum....pg. 35
Swimming at Marie Reed's indoor pool....pg. 74

TOP FIVE DAD/CHILD THINGS TO DO ON A HOT DAY

Upton Hill Regional Park....pg. 85
Cameron Run Regional Park....pg. 83
Swimming at East Potomac Park....pg. 82
Trip to Bethany Beach or Ocean City....pg. 90
Visit one of the Spray Parks....pg. 80

TOP FIVE DAD/CHILD FULL DAY ACTIVITIES

Colonial Williamsburg ....pg. 91
Kings Dominion ....pg. 93
Butler's Orchard..pg. 91
Harper's Ferry ....pg. 93
Adventure Park USA ....pg. 90

TOP FIVE DAD/CHILD SPLURGES $$$

Redskins game at FedEx Field............................pg. 101
Shopping spree at Tugooh toys........................ pg. 56, 67
New outfit at Piccolo Piggies.............................pg. 56
Birthday party at the Corcoran Galley....................pg. 40
Overnight visit to colonial Williamsburg ....pg. 91

TOP FIVE DAD/CHILD MOST MEMORABLE

Nationals game at Nationals Park.........................pg. 101
Leesburg Animal Park ....pg. 93
The Whale and Dino at the Natural History Museum.......pg. 45
Performance at the Kennedy Center ....pg. 41
Boat tour of the monuments ....pg. 96

THE BEST DAD/CHILD RESTAURANTS

JULIE'S EMPANADAS

Adams Morgan

2452 18th St. NW
Washington, DC 20009
(202) 328-6232 | juliasempanadas.com/locations.htm

As this small chain has continued expanding, so have their selections. Empanadas from Central and North America and now also "dessert" empanadas (guava and cream cheese!), at $2 a piece try a bunch!

JUMBO SLICE

Adams Morgan

18th St. NW
Washington, DC 20050
(202) 234-2200

Those who say "never eat anything bigger than your head" have obviously never tried this famous DC pizza joint. The slices are MASSIVE! Each one has its very own box. Split one on the way back from the National Zoo.

SO'S YOUR MOM

Adams Morgan

1831 Columbia Rd. NW
Washington, DC 20009
(202) 462-366

A great place to pick up a bagels and sandwiches for a picnic at nearby Kalorama Park or Walter Pierce Park. Call ahead to place your order and avoid the line! Cash only.

SUPER TACOS

Adams Morgan

1762 Columbia Rd. NW
Washington, DC 20009
(202) 232-7121 | www.supertacosdc.com

The name says it all! All Wonder Dads should join forces with Super Tacos. A California style taqueria that delivers.

THE DINER

Adams Morgan

2453 18th St. NW
Washington, DC 20009
(202) 232-8800 | www.trystdc.com/diner

The kids' classic grilled cheese gets an adult-pleasing upscale spin with gruyere in this restaurant's most popular dish...and don't forget the homefries! (Word on the street is they have the best in town!) This Adams's Morgan favorite gets very busy and the wait can be long. It is best enjoyed with little ones on a quiet Monday night or a weekday breakfast, but they are open 24 hours, if you need grilled cheese at 3 am.

BD'S MONGOLIAN BARBEQUE

Bethesda

7201 Wisconsin Ave.
Bethesda, MD 20814
(301) 657-1080 | www.gomongo.com

Let the kids be their own chef at this noodle restaurant. Do-overs are allowed so is ringing the giant gong.

CAFÉ DELUXE

Bethesda

3228 Wisconsin Ave. NW
Washington, DC 20016
(202) 686-2233 | www.cafedeluxe.com

Gruyere mac and cheese is a must try for parents and kids alike. Thick white paper tablecloths are conducive to doodling or games of tic-tac-toe.

HARD TIMES CAFÉ

Bethesda

4920 Del Ray Ave.
Bethesda, MD 20814
(301) 951-3300 | www.hardtimes.com

A causal neighborhood chili joint. Nothing froo-froo here. Serving no-frills kids' favorites including chicken tenders and burgers. Delicious root beer on tap.

PINES OF ROME

Bethesda

4709 Hampden Ln.
Bethesda, MD 20814
(301) 657-8775

The wonderful food has been the same for years at this classic red-checked table cloth Italian restaurant. The laid back atmosphere is great for lingering conversation and family time on a weekend.

POTBELLY

Bethesda

4731 Elm St.
Bethesda, MD 20810
(240) 497-0150 | www.potbelly.com

A favorite east coast sandwich shop. Great kid's menus and don't forget a milkshake!

CAPITOL CITY BREWING COMPANY

Capitol Hill/Northeast

2 Massachusetts Ave. NE
Washington, DC 20002
(202) 842-2337 | www.capcitybrew.com

State of the art brew houses are located in each restaurant with tours available upon request. Kid friendly menu and atmosphere. Huge soft pretzels with spicy mustard as you wait for your meal! A five minute walk to the Capitol and across the street from historic Union Station.

RESTAURANTS

FOOD COURT AT UNION STATION

Capitol Hill/Northeast

2 West, 40 Massachusetts Ave. NE
Washington, DC 20002
(202) 289-1908 | www.unionstationdc.com

Last time you were at Union Station you may have been rushing to get everyone from Point A to Point B on time. Slow down and enjoy a meal at one of America's most well-loved train stations. With over 50 options in the food court, there is something to please everyone.

GOOD STUFF EATERY

Capitol Hill/Northeast

303 Pennsylvania Ave. SE
Washington, DC 20003
(202) 543-8222 | www.goodstuffeatery.com

Gourmet burgers in Capitol Hill brought to you by Top Chef contestant Spike Mendelsohn. Handspun ice cream too!

MANGIALARDO & SONS

Capitol Hill/Northeast

1317 Pennsylvania Ave. SE
Washington, DC 20003
(202) 543-6212

Amazing weekday lunch spot. Old school Italian deli to a T. Kids and dads alike will love the famous G Man sandwich. Cash only.

THE MARKET LUNCH

Capitol Hill/Northeast

225 7th St. SE
Washington, DC 20003
(202) 547-8444 | www.easternmarket-dc.org

The Market Lunch serves the best breakfast in Capitol Hill. The blueberry pancakes are a must as is a post-breakfast stroll around nearby Eastern Market.

WELLNESS CAFÉ

Capitol Hill/Northeast

325 Pennsylvania Ave. SE
Washington, DC 20003
(202) 543-2266 | www.wellnesscafedc.com

Fresh, flavorful treats on Capitol Hill. Fantastic vegetarian options. Over ten smoothies to choose from.

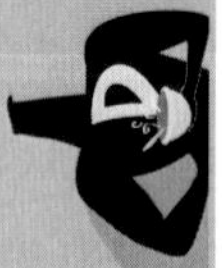

AMERICAN CITY DINER

Chevy Chase/Friendship Heights

5532 Connecticut Ave. NW
Washington, DC 20015
(202) 244-1949 | www.americancitydiner.com

A giant mural of Elvis, Sammy, Davis Jr., James Dean and Marilyn Monroe, amongst chrome and neon make this '50s themed diner a fun place to grab a malt or ice cream soda. Afterwards, catch a few minutes of one of the classic movies screened in the back room.

BOOEYMONGER

Chevy Chase/Friendship Heights

5252 Wisconsin Ave. NW
Washington, DC 20015
(202) 686-5805 | www.booeymonger.com

The funny name will brighten any cranky kid's day! Reasonable prices and a huge selection at this beloved DC sandwich shop. PS. There's a Georgetown location too!

CLYDE'S OF CHEVY CHASE

Chevy Chase/Friendship Heights

5441 Wisconsin Ave
Chevy Chase, MD 20815
(301) 951-9600 | www.clydes.com

The décor in the restaurant features antique cars, trains, and steamships. The restaurant has a large children's menu and the staff is very accommodating of special requests.

COMET PING PONG

Chevy Chase/Friendship Heights

5037 Connecticut Ave. NW
Washington, DC 20008
(202) 364-0404 | www.cometpingpong.com

The wacky name says it all! Personal pizzas with funky toppings and ping pong tables make for a fun family weekend night out.

MAGGIANO'S & CORNER BAKERY

Chevy Chase/Friendship Heights

5333 Wisconsin Ave. NW
Washington, DC 20015
(202) 966-5500 | www.maggianos.com

Meals are served family-style with your pick of two appetizers, two salads, two pasta dishes, and two main courses—enough choices so everyone can have a say! Call 30-45 minutes ahead for seating. Corner bakery (located inside Maggiano's) serves delicious food for all meals. Try the baked French toast for breakfast.

CHINA BOY

Chinatown

817 6th St. NW
Washington, DC 20001
(202) 371-1661

Tucked in a basement with a non-descript sign, China boy offers a great value and the best flat rice noodles around. Fresh soy bean milk is available in bottles.

COCO SALA

Chinatown

929 F St. NW
Washington, DC 20004
(202) 347-4265 | www.cocosala.com

WonderDads and kids alike will love the dessert theme. Don't expect your mother-in-law's bread pudding. Think typical desserts turned on their heads and into a four-course meal.

LEGAL SEAFOODS

Chinatown

704 7th St. NW
Washington, DC 20001
(202) 347-0007 | www.legalseafoods.com

Hit up the Spy Museum then go around the corner for the best crab cakes in DC!

MATCHBOX

Chinatown

713 H St. NW
Washington, DC 20001
(202) 289-4441 | www.matchbox369.com

This "vintage pizza bistro" is located in a historic brick building. Build your own pizza or order off the menu. Also try the mini burgers! In the heart of Chinatown, perfect for a pre or post museum pit stop. Check out the second location in Capitol Hill too!

NANDO'S PERI PERI

Chinatown

819 7th St. NW
Washington, DC 20001
(202) 898-1225 | www.nandosperiperi.com

The popular UK chain has started popping up in the U.S. with its signature succulent chicken and Portuguese rice. The staff gets VERY excited when there's a birthday in the house.

ANGELICO PIZZERIA AND CAFÉ

Cleveland Park/Tenleytown

2313 Wisconsin Ave. NW
Washington, DC 20007
(202) 333-8350 | www.angelicopizzeria.com

Great for a fresh, fast meal. Fast and prompt delivery service makes it great for a Friday night in! Pizza, sandwiches, and calzones.

CACTUS CANTINA

Cleveland Park/Tenleytown

3300 Wisconsin Ave. NW
Washington, DC 20016
(202) 686-7222 | www.cactuscantina.com

Sans bars with the entire restaurant devoted to table-seating, Tex-Mex Cactus Cantina can easily accommodate large parties. The restaurant boasts a "Cowboy and Indian Museum," which displays artifacts and items including antique Stetson hats, headdresses and an 1850s bow-and-arrow set. The National Cathedral is one block north, check out a Behind-the-Scenes Tour or Organ Demonstration after.

THE CEREAL BOWL

Cleveland Park/Tenleytown

3420 Connecticut Ave. NW
Washington, DC 20008
(202) 244-4492 | www.thecerealbowl.com/home.html

Eclectic menu of coffee, cupcakes, ice cream and of course namesake cereal. Cold bowls and hot bowls offer different cereal concoctions, have fun trying to determine the mix or create your own!

TWO AMYS

Cleveland Park/Tenleytown

3715 Macomb St. NW
Washington, DC 20016
(202) 885-5700 | www.2amyspizza.com

Try visiting in off-hours (around 4 or 5pm) to get seated quickly at this very popular Cleveland Park pizza joint. Notoriously family-friendly.

Z BURGER

Cleveland Park/Tenleytown

4321 Wisconsin Ave. NW
Washington, DC 20016
(202) 966-1999 | www.zburger.com

Awesome hand-dipped onion rings and of course burgers. Also offering turkey and veggie burgers with sandwich options.

BEN'S CHILI BOWL
Columbia Heights/U Street Corridor

1213 U St. NW
Washington, DC 20009
(202) 667-0909 | www.benschilibowl.com

A DC landmark. Friendly banter fills the space and many people are regulars. The chili cheese fries are a must. Well-loved by fellow WonderDads Barak Obama and Bill Cosby.

COMMON WEALTH GASTROPUB
Columbia Heights/U Street Corridor

1400 Irving St. NW
Washington, DC 20010
(202) 265-1400 | www.commonwealthgastropub.com

Stop in on Sunday for the Sunday Roast. Starting at 1pm each Sunday, enjoy a family-style Sunday Supper with roast, potatoes, and farm vegetables. After dinner Dad can enjoy a Young's Double Chocolate Stout Float and kids can indulge in a Dominion Root Beer Float.

EL POLLO SABROSO
Columbia Heights/U Street Corridor

1434 Park Rd. NW
Washington, DC 20010
(202) 986-0022

"The Tasty Chicken" lives up to its name. The green sauce is rumored to be addictive. Make sure to get a side of plantain chips. Conveniently located within walking distance of the Columbia Heights metro.

STICKY FINGERS BAKERY
Columbia Heights/U Street Corridor

1370 Park Rd. NW
(202) 299-9700 | www.stickyfingersbakery.com

100% vegan bakery. Delicious treats made with heart healthy soy that are low in saturated fat. Cookies, cupcakes, brownies, muffins, and cakes. Sticky Fingers also serves brunch on the weekends. Vegan and carnivore, Washingtonians love Sticky Fingers.

FUNXION
Downtown

1309 F St. NW
Washington, DC 20004
(202) 386-9466 | www.funxion.com

Healthy (and tasty!) food and beverages designed by an award-winning chef and top nutritionist. FunXion's energy-enhancing meals are a must for any dad on-the-go. Great for breakfast, lunch, and afternoon snacks!

HARD ROCK CAFÉ

Downtown

999 E St. NW
Washington, DC 20004
(202) 737-7625 | www.hardrock.com/washingtondc

Always a crowd pleaser and conveniently located next to Ford's Theatre and across from the FBI building. (Do Journey and J. Edgar Hoover in one afternoon!)

POV AT THE W HOTEL

Downtown

515 15th St. NW
Washington, DC 20004
(202) 661-2400 | www.starwoodhotels.com

The best view in D.C.! Take the kids for lunch and see the White House and monuments from the only rooftop restaurant in D.C.

ROSA MEXICANO

Downtown

575 7th St.
Washington, DC 20004
(202) 783-5522 | www.rosamexicano.info

A fun, festive, atmosphere that works for both children and adults. Great for lunch before a game at the Verizon Center. Be sure to try the guacamole!

BGR THE BURGER JOINT

Downtown

1514 Connecticut Ave. NW
Washington, DC 20036
(202) 299-1071 | www.bgrtheburgerjoint.com

No short-cuts, pre cooking, or heat lamps at this gourment sit-down burger joint. Also serving a variety of milkshakes and floats. The kids meal includes two sliders or a grilled cheese plus fries and a drink!

CREPES A-GO-GO

Downtown

2122 P St. NW
Washington, DC 20050
(202) 955-5655 | www.crepes-a-gogo.com

Anything you want in a Crepe! Let the kids be the chef and pick their own ingredients (even if it ends up being ham, raspberry, and whipped cream with a touch of honey).

FIVE GUYS BURGERS AND FRIES

Downtown

1645 Connecticut Ave. NW
Washington, DC 20009
(202) 328-3483 | www.fiveguys.com

Continuously voted "Best Burger" with Cajun fries to die for. Free peanuts are a plus. "Little" hamburgers and cheeseburgers are available for smaller bellies.

KRAMER BOOKS AND AFTERWARDS CAFÉ

Downtown

1517 Connecticut Ave. NW
Washington, DC 20036
(202) 387-1462 | www.kramers.com

Combine a trip to the bookstore with Sunday brunch. Then head out to the benches in DuPont Circle and read one of your new books together.

PIZZERIA PARADISIO

Downtown

2003 P St. NW
Washington, DC 20036
(202) 223-1245 | www.eatyourpizza.com

Known for their crust, Pizza Paradiso is open seven days a week for lunch and dinner, with continuous service through the afternoon and into the late-night dining hours. Bierra Paradiso was recently added at the DuPont location in response to customers' growing interest in microbrews.

THE FRONT PAGE

Downtown

1333 New Hampshire Ave. NW
Washington, DC 20036
(202) 296-6500 | www.frontpagerestaurant.com

Features famous front pages of various newspapers. The kids will be proud to tell you which pieces of history they know about! Great for lunch or brunch.

FARMERS AND FISHERS

Georgetown

Fountain Level
3000 K St. NW
Washington, DC 20007
(202) 298-0003 | www.farmersandfishers.com

Organic, delicious locally-sourced food. And chocolate- covered bacon lollipops. (Need we say more?)

JETTIES

Georgetown

1609 Foxhall Rd. NW
Washington, DC 20007
(202) 965-3663 | www.jettiesdc.com

A fantastic sandwich spot plain and simple. The Thanksgiving Sandwich is a top seller. Special kids' meal are offered too. Enjoy your lunch outside on the picnic tables out in Jetties' own backyard.

JOHNNY ROCKET'S

Georgetown

3131 M St. NW
Washington, DC 20007
202-333-7994 | www.johnnyrockets.com

Pick out some fun songs together on the juke box at this 1950s themed diner then sit down to fun treats like malted milkshakes and French fries.

LOS CUATES

Georgetown

1564 Wisconsin Ave. NW
Washington, DC 20007
(202) 965-7009 | www.loscuatesrestaurant.com

Family-friendly Tex-Mex. Their queso con carne is renowned city-wide. Delivery and carry out are also available. Walk a block down the street to Thomas Sweet for an after-dinner treat!

OLD GLORY

Georgetown

3139 M St. NW
Washington, DC 20007
(202) 337-3406 | www.oldglorybbq.com

Kids eat free every Sunday and Monday between 5pm-7pm with purchase of adult entrée here at Georgetown's award-winning all American barbeque spot. Over six kinds of barbeque sauce to try!

TACKLEBOX

Georgetown

3245 M St. NW
Washington, DC 20007
(202) 337-8269 | www.tackleboxrestaurant.com

Red and white check tablecloths on picnic benches can make a winter day feel like a fun summer clambake at this Georgetown lobster shack.

BLUE RIDGE RESTAURANT

Glover Park/Palisades/Foxhall

2340 Wisconsin Ave.
Washington, DC 20007
(202) 333-4004 | www.blueridgerestaurant.com

Southern comfort food served in a homey environment. The "meat and potatoes-esque" are sure to please picky eaters. Don't miss Stroller Happy Hour every Thursday from 5pm-7pm featuring a special kids menu!

DC BOATHOUSE

Glover Park/Palisades/Foxhall

5441 MacArthur Blvd. NW
Washington, DC 20016

Cool antique team tee shirts cover the walls. Great pub fare and the Greek owners sure know a thing or two about kabobs!

FIGS FINE FOOD

Glover Park/Palisades/Foxhall

4828 MacArthur Blvd. NW
Washington, DC 20007
(202) 333-7773 | www.figsfinefoodsdc.com

A close walk from Foxhall Playground. Great open faced sandwiches. Head Chef Reem Azoury is known to come out and introduce herself to new faces.

KITCHEN

Glover Park/Palisades/Foxhall

2404 Wisconsin Ave. NW
Washington, DC 20007
(202) 333-3877 | www.kitchen2404.com

Neighborhood comfort food. Customers rave about the macaroni and cheese and burgers are half price on Tuesday.

SURFSIDE

Glover Park/Palisades/Foxhall

2444 Wisconsin Ave
Washington, DC 20007
(202) 337-0004 | www.surfsidedc.com

Kids eat free every Tuesday with purchase of adult entrée. Build your own taco or quesadilla or select from the menu and head upstairs to eat on the roof overlooking Wisconsin Ave..

COMMISSARY

Logan Circle

1443 P St. NW
Washington, DC 20005
Neighborhood: Logan Circle
(202) 299-0018 | www.commissarydc.com

A casual and relaxing café with outdoor seating. Refuel and people watch with some smoothies on the patio after a parent/child yoga class at Flow Yoga.

HOMEMADE PIZZA CO

Logan Circle

522 14th St. NW
Washington, DC 20045
(202) 588-0808 | www.homemadepizza.com

A nice change-up from generic delivery pizza for Friday night. Collaborate on picking out all your own gourmet ingredients and bake your pizza fresh at home.

MID CITY FISH MARKET

Logan Circle

1418 14th St. NW
Washington, DC 20005

If you live in the neighborhood you may have passed right by this place several times–don't let the unassuming exterior fool you! You will be surprised by this great place to satisfy a comfort food hankering. Dishes are filling and perfect for sharing. Whiting fish is excellent with fried rice. (Cash-only).

POSTO

Logan Circle

515 14th St.
Washington, DC 20050
(202) 332-8613 | www.postodc.com

Notorious for its friendly and inviting staff, Posto offers intriguing adult dishes like black truffle fettuccini and familiar kid favorites like cheese tortellini.

SWEETGREEN

Logan Circle

1471 P St. NW
Washington, DC 20005
(202) 234-7336 | www.sweetgreen.com

Fresh, local and healthy design your own salad or wrap then have some froyo for dessert.

LA TASCA

NoVa

2900 Wilson Blvd.
Arlington, VA 22201
(703) 812-9120 | www.latascausa.com

Kids eat free until 6pm on Saturday. With over 45 small plates to try at this restaurant you can feel free to sample a little of everything.

LIBERTY TAVERN

NoVa

3195 Wilson Blvd
Arlington, VA 22201
(703) 465-9360 | www.thelibertytavern.com

Another great brunch buffet. It even includes a kid-pleasing candy section for dessert. For parents—the French press coffee is the best around.

RAY'S HELL BURGER

NoVa

1725 Wilson Blvd
Arlington, VA 22209
(703) 841-0001

The burgers here are pure juicy goodness. Numerous types of root beer and sweet potato fries to die for. The place is small and gets crowded. The craziness can add to the fun, or go on a weeknight for a more laid back vibe.

SILVER DINER

NoVa

3200 Wilson Blvd.
Arlington, VA 22201
(703) 812-8600 | www.silverdiner.com

Huge menu offers a large section of healthy/locally sourced dishes. A large vegetarian selection.

WHITLOW'S ON WILSON

NoVa

2854 Wilson Blvd
Arlington, VA 22209
(703) 276-9693 | www.whitlows.com

A famous all-you-can-eat brunch buffet. The buffet has any and everything you can think of—sure to please any eater! Also open for lunch and dinner.

BRUEGGER'S BAGELS

Penn Quarter/Federal Triangle

509 9th St. NW
Washington, DC 20004
(202) 393-1663 | www.brueggers.com

All the breakfast staples with upscale extras like capers and portabella mushrooms for gourmet dads. Try some of the over ten different kinds of cream cheese. Ample seating to sit and enjoy your breakfast.

CARMINE'S

Penn Quarter/Federal Triangle

425 7th St. NW
Washington, DC 20004
(202) 737-7770 | www.carminesnyc.com

The portions at this casual Italian restaurant are large so be sure to share. The restaurant seats 700 so it is a great idea for groups. For birthdays a giant tiramisu pie can be served for the whole table.

HOT POTATO CAFÉ

Penn Quarter/Federal Triangle

614 E St. NW
Washington, DC 20004
(202) 506-4378 | hotpotatodc.com

A small shop with over a dozen loaded baked potato options. Great stop for carbo-loading for fuel before long walks around all the nearby museums.

TEASIM

Penn Quarter/Federal Triangle

400 8th St. NW
Washington, DC 20004
(202) 638-6010 | www.teaism.com

The salty oatmeal cookies get raves. The Asian-fusion menu will do well with kids who are good eaters. Wide exotic tea selection for the adults.

KIDS RESTAURANT WEEK

www.kidsrestaurantweek.com

Each June for the past three years, the DC area has hosted a Kids Restaurant Week. Kid-friendly fixed price cuisine is offered at DC's favorite restaurants. Kids under 11 pay their age at lunch or early dinner seating between 5pm and 6:30pm with purchase of adult entree. Some restaurants also add additional kid-friendly features for the week including pictures with the chef, cooking demonstrations, and balloon give aways.

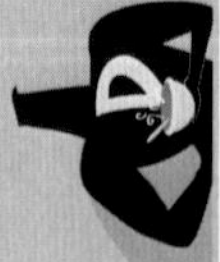

THE BEST DAD/CHILD ACTIVITIES

CRAFTY BASTARDS ARTS AND CRAFTS FAIR

Adams Morgan

Marie Reed Learning Center
18th St. NW
Washington, DC 20009

Lots of funky, shiny, trinkets at this craft fair. Let the kids pick out a hip retro lunchbox then check out the face-painter. Hip dads will love the ironic silk screened tees. Annually in the fall.

CRUMBS AND COFFEE

Adams Morgan

1737 Columbia Rd. NW
Washington, DC 20050
(202) 232-1733

Reliable wireless internet and plenty of plugs make it a cool alternative place for homework time. Stop by in the afternoon for 2 for 1 donuts. Some of the best coffee in Adams Morgan for Dads and hot chocolate for the kids.

DISTRICT OF COLUMBIA ARTS CENTER

Adams Morgan

2438 18th St. NW
Washington, DC 20009
(202) 462-7833 | www.dcartscenter.org

This part black box theatre part galley is non-profit which equals live theatre for cheap! Check the website for kid-friendly plays and storytellers. (FYI the gallery often features avant-garde and controversial exhibits, it may be best to stick on the theatre side).

HELLER'S BAKERY

Adams Morgan

3221 Mt Pleasant St. NW
www.hellersbakery.com

The best Sunday morning donuts. Go early for the most options.

HINCKLEY POTTERY

Adams Morgan

1707 Kalorama Rd. NW
Washington, DC 20009
(202) 745-7055 | www.hinckleypottery.com

Hinckley Pottery offers ten-week sessions for kids. They'll learn to make cups, bowls, and all kinds of neat treasures. If you're lucky they'll make you something!

NATIONAL ZOO

Adams Morgan

3001 Connecticut Ave. NW
Washington, DC 20008
(202) 633-4480 | www.nationalzoo.si.edu

Admission is free at one of the most kid-friendly places to visit in Washington DC. Check the National Zoo blog ahead of visit for information.

PIGMENT ART STUDIO

Adams Morgan

1848 Columbia Rd. NW
Washington, DC 20009
(202) 604-1964

Pigment Art Studio offers classes for kids and adults. (Go across the street to Julia's Empanadas after and see murals done by Manuel the owner!)

STACEY VAETH PHOTOGRAPHY

Adams Morgan

1791 Lanier Pl. NW Ste. 22
Washington, DC 20009
(202) 276-2481 | staceyvaeth.com
Mon-Sun 8 am - 8 pm

Stacey is known for her calm demeanor and great sense of humor. (Many children of DC have been quite smitten with her). Her sessions are adventurous and fun—not endless sedentary posing.

YOGA CHAI

Adams Morgan

1744 Columbia Rd. NW
2nd Floor
Washington, DC 20009
(202) 746-YOGA (9642) | www.yogachai.com

This yoga studio offers all kinds of kids and family classes. Go to a one-time workshop or sign up for a six-week session.

ALL FIRED UP

Bethesda

4923 Elm St.
Bethesda, MD 20814-2905
(301) 654-3206 | www.allfiredupdc.com

Design your own pottery here! This is a companion to the DC location. Their hours vary throughout the year, please call ahead or visit the website to plan.

BE WITH ME PLAYSEUM

Bethesda

7000 Wisconsin Ave
Bethesda, MD
(888) 5PLAYSEUM or (301) 807-8028 | www.playseum.com

The Playseum is a children's used bookstore with plenty of hands-on fun! There are free story and song times, daily art and science activities and plenty of engaging adventures!

BETHESDA ROW CINEMA
Bethesda

7235 Woodmont Ave.
Bethesda, MD 20814
(301) 652-7273 | www.landmarktheatres.com

Independent movie theatre walking distance from the Bethesda metro. The concession stand serves gourmet snacks in addition to the usual Raisinette and slushie treats. Plenty of nearby restaurants and cafes for a meal afterwards.

IMAGINATION STAGE
Bethesda

4908 Auburn Ave
Bethesda, MD 20814
(301) 280-1660 | www.imaginationstage.org

Children's theatre offering programs in acting, filmmaking, dance, and other arts. Imagination Stage also puts on several professional performances for children of all ages. Special workshops are offered for Girl Scouts. Discounts on shows are offered for parties of ten or more so get a group together! The facility can also be rented for parties and events.

JOY OF MOTION DANCE CENTER
Bethesda

Air Rights Building
7315 Wisconsin Ave. Ste. 180E
Bethesda, MD 20814
(301) 986-0016 | www.joyofmotion.org

Dance lessons and summer programs for children of all ages.

LOCUST GROVE NATURE CENTER
Bethesda

In Cabin John Park
777 Democracy Blvd 20817
Bethesda, MD
www.montgomeryparks.org/nature_centers/locust

Interesting, educational, and fun interactive programs for children and parents. Events include story times, nature-themed art projects, and pumpkin and apple picking.

NOW THIS!
Bethesda

Blair Mansion
7111 Eastern Ave.
Silver Spring, MD
(202) 364 8292 | www.nowthisimprov.com

The city's only improvised children's theatre entertains every Sunday with storytelling, jokes, and song.

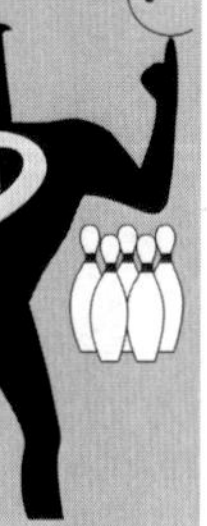

STRATHMORE HALL ARTS CENTER
Bethesda

10701 Rockville Pike
Bethesda, MD 20814
(301) 530-5889 | www.strathmore.org

Plenty of childrens' events. Strathmore Hall is also home to the Maryland Classic Youth Orchestras, the oldest and most established youth orchestra program in the metro area. Children as young as fourth grade are welcome to audition.

STRIKE BETHESDA
Bethesda

5353 Westbard Ave
Bethesda, MD 20816
(301) 652-0955 | www.strikebethesda.com

This isn't your dads bowling alley! Multi-colored pins, dance music, and a cool atmosphere make this much hipper. Go in the afternoon to catch the game on the flat screen TVs while you bowl, and avoid the crowds.

CAPITOL HILL ARTS WORKSHOP
Capitol Hill/Northeast/Southeast

Arts Center
545 7th St. SE
Washington, DC 20003
202-547-6839 | www.chaw.org

Special story times and hands-on activities dedicated especially to little ones. "Read All About It" is a hands-on story time experience where children can get directly involved. The stories are brought to life with small art projects. Make one fish, two fish, red fish, blue fish swim!

NATIONAL POSTAL MUSEUM
Capitol Hill/Northeast/Southeast

2 Massachusetts Ave. NE
Washington, DC 20002
www.postalmuseum.si.edu

Dedicated to the fascinating history of the postal service and the role mail has played in building our nation!

NAVY MUSEUM
Capitol Hill/Northeast/Southeast

805 Kidder Breeze St. SE
Washington, DC 20003
202-433-4882 | www.history.navy.mil

Interactive exhibits commemorate our Navy's wartime heroes and battles. By appointment only.

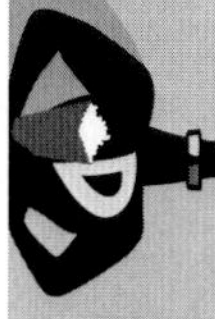

UNION STATION

Capitol Hill/Northeast/Southeast

50 Massachusetts Ave. NE

www.unionstationdc.com

Plenty of shopping, dining, history, and a cool model train exhibit.

UNITED STATES CAPITOL BUILDING

Capitol Hill/Northeast/Southeast

Capitol Hill, east end of National Mall

202-225-6827 | www.aoc.gov

Through films, exhibits, and tours, you will learn about how Congress works, how this magnificent building was built, and how citizens participate in democracy.

SUPREME COURT OF THE UNITED STATES

Capitol Hill/Northeast/Southeast

1st and E Capital Sts. NE

202 479-3030 | www.supremecourtus.gov

Tour the building and attend oral arguments. The gift shop offers educational games and learning aids.

CASA ITALIANA

Chinatown

595½ 3rd St. NW

Washington, DC 2001

(202) 638-1348 | www.casaitalianaschool.com

Childrens' Italian language classes for all levels offered throughout the year. During the summer, various programs in cooking, sports, language, ceramics, art and music.

CHINESE NEW YEAR PARADE

Chinatown

H St. NW & 7th St. NW

Washington, DC 20001

Each year a parade is held in DC's Chinatown to celebrate Chinese New Year. Kids will love the traditional Chinese dragon dance and kung fu demonstrations.

FORD'S THEATRE

Chinatown

511 10th St. NW

Washington, DC 20004

(202) 347-4833 | www.fordtheatre.org

Hear a brief talk by a National Park Ranger about Ford's Theatre and the assassination of Abraham Lincoln. The tour includes a kids'-attention span-friendly thirty-minute one-act play about the events of April 14, 1865. Visits are free, but do require a ticket (which can be reserved online).

LUCKY STRIKE LANES

Chinatown

701 7th St. NW
Washington, DC
(202) 347-1021 | www.bowlluckystrike.com

Sample the fried macaroni and cheese-filled tater tots between frames at this trendy bowling lounge.

MADAME TUSSAUD'S WAX MUSEUM

Chinatown

1001 F St. NW
Washington D.C. 20004
(888) 929-4632 | www.madametussauds.com

Catch Grover Cleveland and Rhianna in the same afternoon! This museum is full of creepy-good wax likenesses of presidents, pop stars, and other people of note.

MARTIN LUTHER KING JR. LIBRARY

Chinatown

901 G St. N.W.
202-727-0321 | www.dclibrary.org/MLK

Storytimes, baby/toddler socialization sessions, and various children's workshops.

NATIONAL BUILDING MUSEUM

Chinatown

401 F St. NW
Washington DC 20001
(202) 272 2448 | www.nbm.org

Several kid-friendly interactive exhibits. Pick up your own "tool kit" when you arrive full of cool things to help you explore the museum! The Building Zone makes a cool birthday party spot. Check the website for several family-friendly workshops offered throughout the year.

NATIONAL MUSEUM OF CRIME AND PUNISHMENT

Chinatown

575 7th St. NW
Washington, DC 20004
(202) 621-5567 | http://www.crimemuseum.org

From Genghis Kahn to Gordon Gekko we are a culture fascinated by criminals. Kids will love a hands-on "CSI lab" where they can solve their own crime. Dads can check out an FBI shooting range. Stop by and see the studio where "America's Most Wanted" is filmed. If the kids have been unruly lately take them by the replica jail cell! Hours vary by season, call or check the website for information.

SPY MUSEUM

Chinatown

800 F St. NW
Washington, DC 20004
(202) 393-7798 | www.spymuseum.org

The Spy Museum will be your guide to "clandestine stories, covert ops, self-destructing memos, lipstick pistols and more." The Spy Museum offers special workshops for kids and families, including one on how to be a master of disguise! Check the website for details.

VERIZON CENTER

Chinatown

601 F St. NW
Washington, DC 20004
(202) 628-3200

Home to the NHL's Capitals, NBA's Wizards, and WNBA's Mystics. It also hosts Georgetown University men's basketball, concerts and various other performances.

ALL FIRED UP

Cleveland Park/Tenleytown/Van Ness

3413 Connecticut Ave. NW
Washington, DC 20008
(202) 363-9590 | www.allfiredupdc.com

Unlimited studio time so you can truly relax and paint at this do-it-yourself pottery studio. All glazes are non toxic and lead free. Great birthday party packages.

HILLWOOD MUSEUM AND GARDENS

Cleveland Park/Tenleytown/Van Ness

4155 Linnean Ave. NW
Washington, DC 20008
(202) 686-5807 | www.hillwoodmuseum.org

One of the most overlooked museums in DC. This off-the-beaten path mansion is the restored and very intact estate of Post cereal fortune heiress Marjorie Merriweather Post. Unique and fascinating treasures inside the home (some rescued from Stalin who had stolen them in an attempt to raise money for industrialization), beautiful gardens outside. Tours by reservation only.

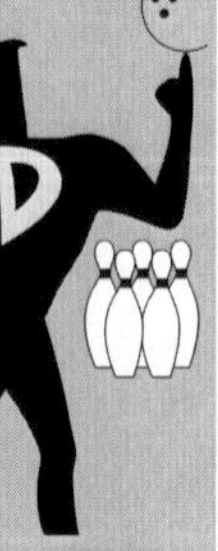

NATIONAL MUSEUM OF HEALTH AND MEDICINE

Cleveland Park/Tenleytown/Van Ness

6900 Georgia Ave.
Washington, DC 20307
(202) 782-2200 | www.nmhm.washingtondc.museum

A great hidden gem museum for curious minds interested in the human body. See human specimens, antique medical instruments, and artifacts from the Lincoln assassination. If you drive, you'll need your license, registration, and proof of insurance to get into the complex. All adults will need to show proper state ID as well.

THE UPTOWN
Cleveland Park/Tenleytown/Van Ness

3426 Connecticut Ave. NW
Washington, DC 20008
(202) 966-8805

Historic deco single screen movie theatre provides a cool alternative to the mega-plex. Plays new releases.

US NAVAL OBSERVATORY
Cleveland Park/Tenleytown/Van Ness

Massachusetts Ave. NW & Observatory Cir. NW
Washington, DC 20008
www.usno.navy.mil

Public tours are offered on selected Monday evenings. Tours include a presentation and explanation of the master clock system and star gazing through a high powered telescope with a professional astronomer. Tours fill up fast so scheduling ahead of time is highly recommended.

BLACK FASHION MUSEUM
Columbia Heights/U Street Corridor

2007 Vermont Ave. NW
Washington, DC 20001
(202) 667-0744

Major DC hidden gem. View African-American's contributions to the fashion-world. By appointment only.

BLOOMBARS
Columbia Heights/U Street Corridor

3222 11th St. NW
Washington, DC 20010
www.bloombars.com

BloomBars is an uplifting and energetic boutique performance space that offers storytelling and art workshops for kids of all ages.

COLUMBIA HEIGHTS COMMUNITY CENTER
Columbia Heights/U Street Corridor

1480 Girard St. NW
Washington, DC 20009
(202) 671-0373

Play a game of HORSE or knockout at the community center's indoor or outdoor basketball courts. The outdoor ones are lighted so an early evening game can be a fun after-dinner outing. Check the website for various youth programs offered throughout the year.

FROZENYO

Columbia Heights/U Street Corridor

3237A 14th St. NW
Washington, DC 20010
www.frozenyo.com

10+ flavors and dozens of toppings let kids be the artist behind their own treat.

JOSEPHINE BUTLER PARKS CENTER

Columbia Heights/U Street Corridor

2437 15th St. NW
Washington, DC 20009
(202) GO-2-PARK (202-462-7275)
www.washingtonparks.net/parkscenter.html

The Parks Center often hosts family-friendly bike rides throughout the city.

MT. PLEASANT FARMER'S MARKET

Columbia Heights/U Street Corridor

Lamont Park at 17th St. NW
Washington, DC 20010
(410) 303-0864 | www.MtPFM.org

This farmer's market posts their available crops online and offers corresponding recipes. Pick one out together beforehand then go shop for the goods! Saturday 9am-1pm in Lamont Park at the corner of 17th & Lamont Streets, NW. The market runs from May through November.

TIVOLI THEATRE

Columbia Heights/U Street Corridor

3333 14th St. NW
Washington, DC 20010
(202) 234-7174 | www.galatheatre.org

This beautiful landmark building is home to GALA Hispanic Theatre and several retail shops and restaurants.

BEDAZZLED

DuPont Circle

1507 Connecticut Ave. NW
Washington, DC 20036
(202) 265-232 | www.bedazzled.net

The perfect accompaniment to a trip to the Textile Museum. Let the little fashionista select her own beads to make a gorgeous necklace, bracelet, or other bead project.

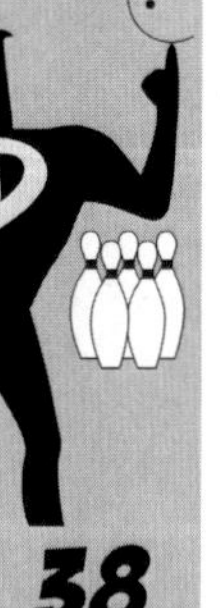

BREWMASTER'S CASTLE

DuPont Circle

1307 New Hampshire Ave.
Washington, DC 20036
(202) 429-1894 | www.heurichhouse.org

One of Washington's best-kept secrets. In one of the country's most intact Victorian houses brewer and philanthropist Chrisitan Heurich also built one of the nation's first "smart homes," complete with fireproofing, secret passages, and more.

DUPONT CIRCLE MEMORIAL FOUNTAIN

DuPont Circle

DuPont Circle
Washington, DC 20036

Named in honor of Civil War naval hero, Samuel Francis DuPont, the fountain is the largest in the city and an awesome place to sit and relax during a day about town. A great place to take an ice cream cone or a snack to go so the kids can climb on you without spilling on others.

FONDO DEL SOL VISUAL ARTS CENTER

DuPont Circle

2112 R St. NW
Washington, DC 20008
(202) 483-2777 | www.dkmuseums.com/fondo.html

Devoted to Latin American, Native American, and Caribbean culture this museum also features bilingual education programs for children.

HELLO! CUPCAKE

DuPont Circle

1351 Connecticut Ave. NW
Washington DC 20036
(202) 861-2253 www.hellocupcakeonline.com

Stop by for a delicious treat after visiting DuPont's numerous galleries. Try the "Raspberry Beret" (not the kind you find in a second-hand store), the Peppermint Penny, or a Vanilla Gorilla.

THE PHILLIPS COLLECTION

DuPont Circle

1600 21st St. NW
Washington, DC 20009
(202) 387-2151 | www.phillipscollection.org

America's first modern art museum. No charge for visitors under 18. Kids will love the funky Matisses.

TEXTILE MUSEUM

DuPont Circle

2320 S St. NW
Washington, DC 20008
(202) 667-0441 | www.textilemuseum.org

Perfect for your junior fashionista! Featuring clothing from all the way back to 3000 BC (almost as long ago as acid-washed jeans). There's a hand-on room where you can learn some of the science behind the textile business. See (and touch!) a silk worm cocoon.

NATIONAL MUSEUM OF AMERICAN JEWISH MILITARY HISTORY

DuPont Circle

1811 R St. NW
Washington, DC 20008
(202) 265-6280 | ww.nmajmh.org

Cool memorabilia from American military conflicts on display. The "Hidden Treasures" exhibit features a wealth of cool mementos and is a must-see.

THE CORCORAN GALLEY

Downtown

Corcoran College of Art + Design
500 17th St. NW
Washington, DC 20006

Aspiring artist classes for children as young as five. The Corcoran offers a cultural and cool kids' birthday party package consisting of private docent tour, hand-on art project, goody bag, and to Dad's relief—someone to help supervise.

DAUGHTERS OF THE AMERICAN REVOLUTION MUSEUM

Downtown

1776 D St. NW
Washington, DC 20006
(202) 879-3241 | www.dar.org/museum

There are more than thirty period-decorated rooms in this historic mansion. Little girls will love the attic filled with antique toys and dolls.

VARIOUS SMITHSONIAN MUSEUMS

Downtown

Features live performances throughout the Smithsonian network for young audiences. Puppet shows, sing-alongs, science demonstrations, and up-close-and-personal time with some of the coolest animals. Everything is educational!

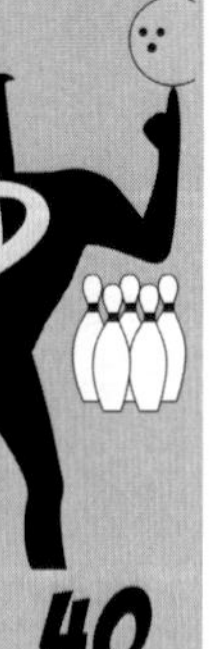

THE KENNEDY CENTER

Downtown

2700 F St.

(202) 467-4600 | www.kennedy-center.org

Lots of shows for young audiences including old favorites and original performances.

THE NATIONAL AQUARIUM

Downtown

1401 Constitution Ave. NW

Washington, DC 20230

(202) 485-2825 | www.national aquariam.org

Go check out the Boneytail Chub, Gineaufowl Puffer and the False Map Turtle (with family vote on which one is the ugliest is optional). A trip to the National Aquarium is best coupled up with a visit to the nearby Washington Monument. Daily animal feedings and aquarist talks at 2 pm.

NATIONAL GEOGRAPHIC MUSEUM

Downtown

1145 17th St. NW

Washington, DC 20036

(202) 857-7588 | www.nationalgeographic.com

Cool rotating exhibits. National Geographic Live! Offers concerts, demonstrations, and screenings.

THE OCTAGON MUSEUM

Downtown

1799 New York Ave. NW

Washington, DC 20006

(202) 626 7318 | www.archfoundation.org/octagon

Designed by the first architect of the United States Capitol, William Thorton, the Octagon was home to the American Institute of Architects for several years. Check the website for cool exhibits and programs.

THE WHITE HOUSE

Downtown

1600 Pennsylvania Ave.

Washington, DC 20500

(202) 456-1414 | www.whitehouse.gov

How could you miss this?! The Easter Egg Roll is a beloved annual spring event. Tickets are available online via a lottery system.

THE BOAT HOUSE AT FLETCHER'S COVE

Georgetown

4940 Canal Rd. NW
Washington, DC 20007
(202) 244-0461 | www.fletcherscove.com

Rent a canoe, kayak or rowboat. You can even pick up bait or buy a fishing license inside the Tackle Shack. Stop off at the Georgetown waterfront for some food after!

BRUSH 'N BLUSH

Georgetown

3210 Grace St.
Washington DC, 20007
(202) 338-1705 | www.brush-n-blush.com

This paint studio lets anyone be an artist! Check the calendar online for "family days' where you and little ones can paint Winnie the Pooh or fun holiday pictures together.

DUMBARTON OAKS

Georgetown

1703 32nd St. NW
Washington, DC 20007
(202) 339-6401 | www.doaks.org

A relaxing respite in the middle of the city. Relax in the gardens (picnicking is allowed in nearby Montrose Park) and tour the museum. Seasonal hours vary, call ahead to confirm.

GEORGETOWN CUPCAKE

Georgetown

3301 M St. NW
Washington, DC 20007

After your picnic at the Old Stone House, stop by Georgetown Cupcake for a world-famous treat.

HAAGEN-DAZS

Georgetown

3201 M St. NW
Washington, DC 20007
(202) 333-3443 | www.haagen-dazs.com

The well-known favorite has an outfit in Georgetown featuring a cool mural map of locations of the homes of celebrities who have called the area home.

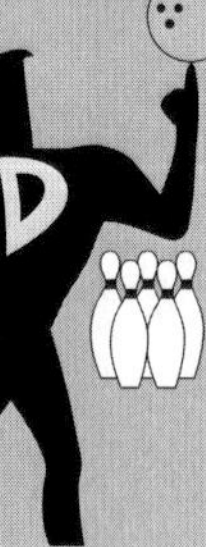

THE OLD STONE HOUSE

Georgetown

3501 M St. NW
Washington, DC 2007

This unassuming 18th century cottage is one of the oldest remaining structures in the nation's capital. Tour the cottage then picnic in the backyard!

THOMPSON BOAT CENTER

Georgetown

2900 Virginia Ave. NW
Washington, DC 20007
(202) 333-9543 | www.thompsonboatcenter.com

More canoe, kayak, rowboat, and sailboat rentals, plus bikes too! Open late Spring to Fall.

JONAH'S TREEHOUSE

Glover Park/Palisades/Foxhall

2121 Wisconsin Ave. NW
Washington, DC 20007
(202) 298-6805 | www.jonahstreehouse.com

Jonah's Treehouse offers a wide range of play and movement classes for babies, toddlers, and preschoolers. The ball pit is always a crowd pleaser.

NATIONAL CATHEDRAL

Glover Park/Palisades/Foxhall

3101 Wisconsin Ave. NW
Washington, DC 20016
(202) 537-6200 | www.nationalcatherdral.org

Take a family scavenger hunt! The cathedral provides a guide to help you find stained glass windows, tiny carvings, wrought iron animals, and gargoyles. You can also listen to the bells on the South Lawn or in the Bishop's Garden.

ROCK CREEK PARK HORSE CENTER

Glover Park/Palisades/Foxhall

5100 Glover Rd.
Washington, DC 20015
(202) 363-8767 | www.rockcreekhorsecenter.com

Be a hero and accommodate the repeated birthday and Christmas gift requests for "a pony." 10-15 minute rides can be scheduled in advance for children ages 2 ½ and up. The "Ponies and Friends" Camp is geared towards 4-7 year olds and runs for one week sessions throughout the summer. The camp runs in the evening.

ROCK CREEK PARK NATURE CENTER AND PLANETARIUM

Glover Park/Palisades/Foxhall

5200 Glover Rd. NW
Washington DC 20015
(202) 895 6700 | www.nps.gov/rocr

Guided walks on weekends and plenty of hands-on activities for kids.

CHILDREN'S STUDIO SCHOOL

Logan Circle

1301 V St. NW
Washington, DC 20009
(202) 387-6148 | www.studioschool.org

Children's Studio School is a full-time day school that also offers summer programs for non-students. City Studio is six-week summer program where young participants work with architects, artists, and writers to explore Washington D.C. Students act as historians, poets, and urban planners.

THE STUDIO THEATRE

Logan Circle

1501 14th St. NW
Washington, DC 20005
(202) 332-3300 | www.studiotheatre.org

The Young Actors Ensembles program introduces young people to acting. For registration information, visit their website.

FRESHFARM MARKETS

Penn Quarter/Federal Triangle

8th St. NW between D and E Sts. NW
Washington, DC 200036
www.freshfarmmarket.org

Local farmers sell fruits, vegetables, cheeses, breads, cookies, meat, and flowers. Let kids pick out their own mix of fruit and make smoothies at home. From April to December.

ICE RINK AT THE SCULPTURE GARDEN

Penn Quarter/Federal Triangle

7th St. and Constitution Ave.
Washington, DC
(202) 289-3360 | www.pavillioncafe.com/ice_rink.html

View the magnificent sculptures while gliding on the ice. A state-of-the-art sound system pipes in background music. Warm up with hot chocolate in the café after. "Snow Plow Sam" group classes available for children of all ages as are private lessons.

NATIONAL ARCHIVES

Penn Quarter/Federal Triangle

700 Pennsylvania Ave. NW
Washington, DC 20408
www.archives.gov

Perfect for junior history buffs! The Rotunda of the National Archives Building houses the permanent exhibit of the Constitution, Bill of Rights, and the Declaration of Independence.

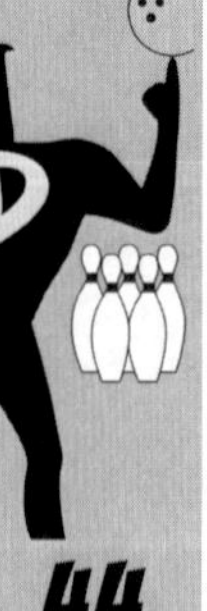

NATIONAL MUSEUM OF NATURAL HISTORY

Penn Quarter/Federal Triangle

10th St. & Constitution Ave. NW
Washington, DC 20560
(202) 633-1000 | www.mnh.si.edu

With a collection of 124 million objects (even more than your parents' last yard sale), this place surely has something for everyone. Check out the new endangered plants exhibit. Also don't miss the T-Rex skeleton and the whale! Also Dads—there's an IMAX theatre. (We know you want to see it in IMAX too).

NATIONAL PORTRAIT GALLERY

Penn Quarter/Federal Triangle

8th and F Sts. NW
Washington, DC 20001
Daily 11:30 am-7:00 pm
(202) 633-8300 | www.npg.si.edu

Not just a bunch of boring paintings! People who have shaped American history (even the villains) are portrayed via visual and performing art and new media. Share the stories of our country's history, and great art, with your kids!

NEWSUEM

Penn Quarter/Federal Triangle

555 Pennsylvania Ave. NW
Washington, DC 20001
(202) 292-610 | www.newseum.org

Kids will love the NBC interactive newsroom that lets them put together their own broadcast. The Pulitzer Prize Photographs Galley will wow everyone.

WARNER THEATRE

Penn Quarter/Federal Triangle

1299 Pennsylvania Ave. NW
Washington, DC 20004
www.warnertheatre.com

This beautiful historic theatre was built as a movie house in the 1920s. Check the website for plenty of age-appropriate shows.

ALEXANDRIA ARCHEOLOGY MUSEUM

NoVa

105 N. Union St.
Alexandria, VA 2314
(703) 746-4399 | www.oha.alexandria.gov

Combine with a trip to the Torpedo Factory. Make a reservation for a "Dig Day" where kids are invited to help city archeologist sift through earth for artifacts.

ARLINGTON NATIONAL CEMETERY NoVa

Arlington, VA 22211

Arlington National Cemetery has several special points of interest including the Eternal Flame of the Kennedy Grave and the mast of the USS Maine.

BOCCATO GELATO & ESPRESSO NoVa

2719 Wilson Blvd
Arlington, VA 22201
(703) 869-6522 | boccato.com

With a larger than average list of flavors (mojito, chocolate Guinness) there is something to please everyone! Grab a cup to go after dinner and sit out on the benches outside. Some also say it's the best cup of coffee in Arlington. Cash only.

CLARK STREET PLAYHOUSE NoVa

601 S Clark St.
Arlington, VA 22202
(703) 418-4808 | www.washingtonshakespeare.org

Local theatre with intimate feel. Did you know DC is second only to New York City in terms of number of professional theatre companies?

COLUMBIA ISLAND MARINA NoVa

George Washington Memorial Pkwy.
Arlington, VA 2202
(202) 347-0713 | www.columbiaisland.com

The marina offers catering for a unique birthday party or family picnic. For Dads who boat Columbia Island Marina is the perfect place to enter the Potomac for fishing or cruising.

FRIENDSHIP FIREHOUSE NoVa

107 S Alfred St.
Alexandria, VA 22314
(703) 838-3891

Little kids will be red hot for this teeny-tiny firehouse that is now a museum.

KETTLER CAPITALS ICEPLEX NoVa

627 N Glebe Rd.
Arlington, VA 22203
(571) 224-0555 | www.kettlercapitalsiceplex.com

Washington Capital practices are open to the public. The ice is open to public skating each day. Kettler Capitals Iceplex is also home to several youth hockey leagues.

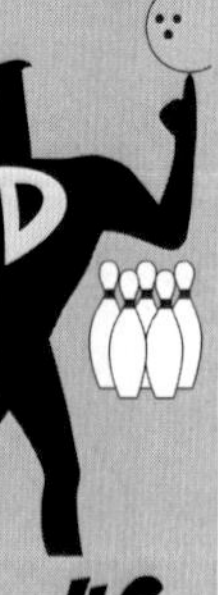

KH ART & FRAMING
NoVa

4745 Lee Hwy.
Arlington, VA 22207
(703) 525-6132 | www.khartframing.com

Beautiful and reasonably priced framing jobs. Little ones will get a thrill out of designing a professional frame for their masterpiece.

MARKET SQUARE
NoVa

301 King St.
Alexandria, VA 22314

The nation's oldest farmers market. Fresh goodies and crafts! Get some fresh fruits and veggies to make a healthy weekend breakfast.

SIGNATURE THEATRE
NoVa

4200 Campbell Ave
Arlington, VA 22206
(703) 820-9771 | www.signature-theatre.org

Beloved local theatre. Check the website for kid-friendly performances and workshops.

SPORTROCK CLIMBING CENTER
NoVa

5308 Eisenhower Ave.
Alexandria, VA
703 212 7625 | www.sportrock.com

Classes to teach kids to climb! Kids have free rein of the place from 6:30pm-8pm.

SUR LA TABLE
NoVa

1101 S Joyce St. # B20
Arlington, VA 22202-2065
(703) 414-3580 | www.surlatable.com

Well organized, small and fun cooking classes for kids as young as 6!

STABLER-LEADBEATHER APOTHECARY MUSEUM
NoVa

105-107 S. Fairfax St.
703-838-4200 | www.apothecarymuseum.org

Mystery potions remain intact in this old Quaker pharmacy now a museum. George and Martha Washington were customers.

TORPEDO FACTORY ART CENTER

NoVa

105 N. Union St.
Alexandria, VA 2314
703- 838- 4565 | www.torpedofactory.org

A former United States Navy torpedo plant now is now home to this permanent arts and crafts fair.

ANNUAL CHERRY BLOSSOM FESTIVAL AND PARADE

Southwest

March 26th -April 10th 2011
Parade is April 8th
www.nationalcherryblossomfestival.org

The National Park Service sponsor "Bloomin Junior Ranger Days" during the Festival. Kids and parents alike will love hearing about the history of the cherry blossom trees. Various art, fashion, culture, and educational events are also offered. Another neat event is the Guided Ranger Lantern Tour—explore the cherry blossoms at night.

ARENA STAGE

Southwest

1101 6th St. SW
Washington, DC 20024
(202) 488-4377 | www.arenastage.org

Specializing in new and classic American plays. If you have a little one who loves to ham it up, bring them to the theater to be inspired by the pros.

MAINE AVE. FISH MARKET

Southwest

1100 Maine Ave. SW
Washington DC 20024
(202) 484-2722

Visit with the friendly fishermen and let the kids select their own bivalve, crustacean, or pesca to prepare at home!

NATIONAL AIR AND SPACE MUSEUM

Southwest

Independence Ave. at 6th St. SW
Washington, DC 20560
202-633-2214 | www.nasm.si.edu

Hundreds of historic artifacts on display here including the Wright Brothers 1903 Flyer; the Spirit of St. Louis and the Apollo 11 spaceship, Columbia. WonderDads can take kids to the moon thanks to a lunar rock sample that visitors can touch! Check out the flight simulator too. The Albert Einstein Planetarium has two shows daily. How Things Fly is a favorite gallery amongst children. Sign up for a paper-airplane contest.

NATIONAL MALL/SMITHSONIAN MERRY-GO-ROUND

Southwest

1000 Jefferson Dr. SW
Washington DC 20560

Hot dogs and a merry-go-round without the hassle of your typical "mall." Let the kids run free on the mall (feel free to bring Frisbees, balls, and bikes).

THE NATIONAL MUSEUM OF THE AMERICAN INDIAN

Southwest

4th St. and Independence Ave. SW
Washington, DC 20024
202 633 1000 | www.nmai.si.edu

Plenty of hands-on activities. Cultural interpreters are available throughout the museum to offer information in kid-friendly 5-15 minute spurts on topics such as animals, dolls, and containers. Also check out hok-noth-da (did you hear?) daily at 11:30am. Join museum staff to explore Native American culture through storytelling and tactile experience.

ODYSSEY CRUISES

Southwest

600 Water St. SW
Washington, DC 20024
(866) 306-2469 | www.odysseycruises.com

Bring the whole family aboard for a brunch cruise and have an awesome view of monuments from the water! The wide buffet selection is sure to please any palette. Children under three are free and those three to eleven are half price.

TIDAL BASIN PADDLE BOATS

Southwest

1501 Maine Ave. SW
Washington, DC 2024
(202) 479 2426 | www.tidalbasinpaddleboats.com

Advanced group reservations available Monday-Friday, 10am-4pm. Take a break from touring the monuments and relax in the sun from your very own paddle boat. Enjoy view of the Japanese Cherry trees and Jefferson Memorial. Pre-registration guarantees a boat but is not necessary. If there is a wait, browse the souvenir vendors at the Washington Monument.

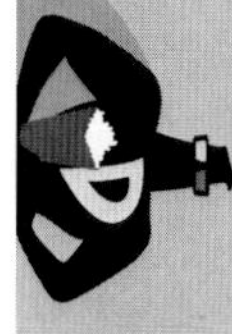

UNITED STATES BUREAU OF ENGRAVING AND PRINTING

Southwest

14th and C St. SW
Washington, DC 20228
(202) 874-2330 | www.moneyfactory.gov

Show the kids that money does not grow on trees after all. Free, same-day tour tickets are distributed at 8 a.m. on a first-come, first-served basis at the ticket booth on Raoul Wallenberg Place (formerly 15th St.). Lines form early and tickets go quickly, usually by 9 a.m. Tours run every 15 minutes from 9 to 10:45 a.m. and 12:30 to 2 p.m.

THE US HOLOCAUST MEMORIAL MUSEUM: DANIEL'S STORY

Southwest

1000 Raul Wallenberg Pl SW
202- 488-0400 | www.ushm.org

Children ages eight and above are invited to a special exhibit, "Remember the Children: Daniel's Story." It tells the story of the Holocaust through the eyes of an 8 year old Jewish boy. The permanent collection is not recommended for children under the age of eleven.

WASHINGTON MONUMENT

Southwest

State Pl NW
Washington, District of Columbia 20006
(202) 426-6841 | www.nps.gov/wamo

Take the elevator to the top. Kids will love the birds-eye view of the nation's capital.

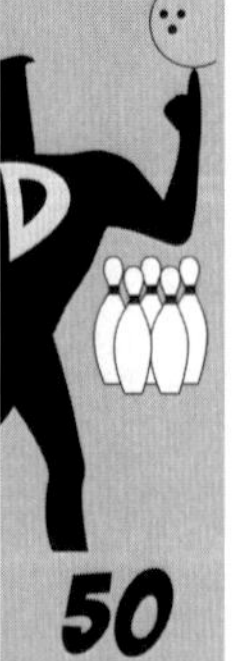

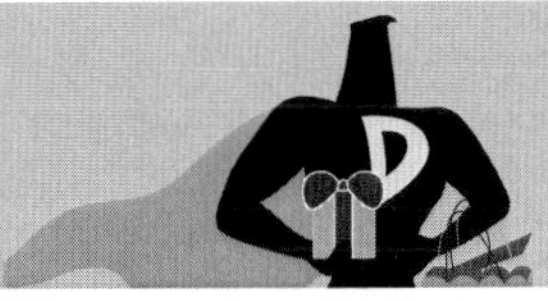

THE BEST DAD/CHILD STORES

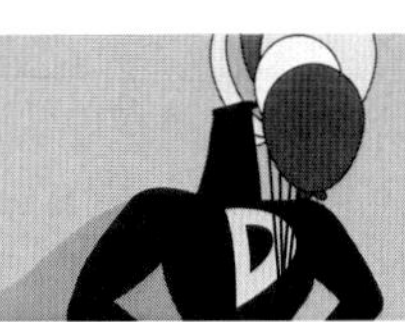

BAZAAR ATLAS

Adams Morgan

2405 18th St. NW
Washington, DC 20009
(202) 332-4911

Curious curios and interesting imports. Interesting art and knick-knacks from around the world.

CITY BIKES

Adams Morgan

2501 Champlain St. NW
Washington, DC 20009
(202) 265-1564 | www.citybikes.com

This friendly neighborhood bike shop is known to do many minor fixes free of charge.

CROOKED BEAT RECORDS

Adams Morgan

2318 18th St. NW
Washington, DC 20009
(202) 483-2328

Great collection of hard-to-find viynls. A great field trip after WonderDad rock-and-roll history lessons on the home stereo.

IDLE TIME BOOKS

Adams Morgan

2467 18th St. NW
Washington, DC 20009
(202) 232-4774

Funky used bookstore with a wide and random selection. Find a few classic childrens' books to read aloud together.

MEEPS VINTAGE FASHIONETTE

Adams Morgan

2104 18th St. NW
Washington, DC 20009
(202) 265-6546

Solid collection of men's vintage clothing. Have fun playing dress up with the kids. (And maybe even come home with a cool blue velvet jacket or vintage concert tee).

MERCEDES BIEN VINTAGE

Adams Morgan

2423 18th St. NW
Washington, DC 20009
(202) 360-8481

The most radical clothes in D.C. Worth taking a peak, for the shock value, or to educate your little princess in the avant-garde.

OYA'S MINI BAZAAR

Adams Morgan

2420 18th St. NW
Washington, DC 20009
(202) 667-9853

A global selection of mini beads and trinkets. Shopping feels like a treasure hunt.

SKYNEAR & COMPANY

Adams Morgan

2122 18th St. NW
Washington, DC 20009
(202) 797-7160 | www.skynearonline.com

If your considering letting little one's have a hand in decorating their own room, Skynear's "design your own sofa" option may be for you! Also, a wide selection of kid-friendly plastic furniture.

TIBET SHOP

Adams Morgan

2407 18th St. NW
Washington, DC 20009
(202) 387-1880

Tables with little crafts and jewelry for $5 owned by an award-winning Tibetan photographer. Beautiful handmade pieces as well.

TORO MATA

Adams Morgan

2410 18th St. NW
Washington, DC 20009
(202) 232-3890

All the pieces have a unique story at this Adam's Morgan arts and crafts gallery.

WESTERN MARKET

Adams Morgan

2200 Champlain St. NW
Washington, DC 20009
(202) 299-7358
Saturdays Only

A new arts and crafts market along the lines of Capitol Hill's Eastern Market. Stroll through on a Saturday then hit up your favorite Adam's Morgan lunch spot. Paintings, photography, pottery, glassware, handbags, and hand-woven clothing.

VINTAGE NO. 5

Adams Morgan

2704½ Ontario Rd. NW
Washington, DC 20009

Your petite fashionista will go crazy over the wide selection of vintage hats.

ANGLO-DUTCH POOLS AND TOYS

Bethesda

5460 Westbard Ave.
Bethesda, MD 20816
(301) 951-0636 | www.anglodutchpoolsandtoys.com

Great selection of pool, beach, and popular favorite toys. The store also has a sporting goods section. Full stock of pool supplies and equipment.

BIG PLANET COMICS

Bethesda

4908 Fairmont Ave.
Bethesda, MD 20814
(301) 654-6856

Offers independent and alternative hip comics. Special section devoted to children's comics.

KIDVILLE

Bethesda

4825 Bethesda Ave.
Bethesda, MD 20814
(301) 656-5030 | www.kidville.com

So much in one location! A kid friendly hair-salon plus boutique. The boutique has all the latest fashions for the six and under set. Kids can sit and relax during their haircut with games, toys, or a DVD.

PICCOLO PIGGIES

Bethesda

10231 Old Georgetown Rd.
Bethesda, MD 20814
(301)493-0123 | www.piccolo-piggies.com

The cutest kids clothes in town including mini-me sized Lilly Pultizer and Ralph Lauren. All ages from baby to ten. The second floor is dedicated to party dresses. Cool dad-friendly diaper bags too!

WIGGLEROOM

Bethesda

4924 Del Ray Ave.
Bethesda, MD 20814
(301)656.5995 | www.wiggleroom.biz

Infant, children, and maternity consignment shop featuring quality labels. The store also carries baby gear and toys.

YIRO/TUGOOH TOYS

Bethesda

823 Bethesda Ave.
Bethesda, MD 20814
(301)654.2413 | www.yirostores.com

Natural, education, eco-friendly and FUN toys you can believe in giving to your kids.

BACKSTAGE, INC. THE PERFORMING ARTS STORE

Capitol Hill

545 8th St. SE
Washington, DC 20003
(202) 544-5744 | backstagebooks.com

They have everything you need to meet your crazy costuming or dress up needs!

CAPITOL HILL BOOKS

Capitol Hill

657 C St. SE
Washington, DC 20003
(202) 544-1621 | www.capitolhillbooks-dc.com

Books here, books there, books are EVERYWHERE (even in the bathroom!) at this little independent bookshop. You will also find humorous little notes directing you throughout the store.

DAWN PRICE BABY

Capitol Hill

325 7th St. SE
Washington, DC 20003
(202) 543-2920 | www.dawnpricebaby.com

Super knowledgeable and friendly sales staff knows their stuff on all products baby. They have it all at this beautiful boutique: toys, trinkets, onesies, strollers, and high chairs. Great place to get an outfit for a special occasion.

FAIRY GODMOTHER CHILDREN'S' BOOKS AND TOYS

Capitol Hill

319 7th St. SE
Washington D.C., District of Columbia 20003
(202) 547-5474

Plenty of cute merchandise in this tiny unique and eccentric boutique.

GROOVYLAND

Capitol Hill

425 8th St. SE
Washington, DC 20003
(202) 544-7474 | www.groovydc.com

Plenty of toys, games, and novelties. Great party supply section including a great selection of balloons!

MONKEY'S UNCLE

Capitol Hill

323 7th St. SE
Washington, DC 20003
(202) 543-6471 | monkeysuncleonthehill.com

Buy and sell cute clothes for kids of all ages at this green boutique. Clean out the closets and make some money for a fun activity!

STORES

RIVERBY BOOKS

Capitol Hill

417 E Capitol St. SE
Washington, DC 20003
(202) 543-4342 | www.riverbybooks.com

Tons of kids books in the basement and free tea on chilly days! There is also a small pottery and jewelry selection. Be sure to check out the $1 books table!

STITCH DC

Capitol Hill

731 8th St. SE
Washington, DC 20003
(202) 544-8900 | www.stitchdc.com

A great place to have an arts and crafts birthday party! The shop also sells training knitting needles that are perfect for young crafters!

TOY SOLIDER SHOP

Capitol Hill

503 11th St. SE
Washington, DC 20003
(202) 546 2201 | www.oysolidershop.com

A MAJOR hidden gem just blocks from the Capitol. The Toy Solider Shop is located on the bottom floor of a restored row house and displays several thousand antique toy soldiers along with books and vintage World War II posters.

BARSTON'S CHILD PLAY

Chevy Chase/Friendship Heights

5536 Connecticut Ave. NW
Washington, DC 20015
(202) 244-3602

Huge selection of educational (and fun!) toys for all ages. Plenty of children's accessories ranging from car seats and strollers to furniture.

FULL OF BEANS

Chevy Chase/Friendship Heights

5502 Connecticut Ave. NW
Washington, DC 20015
(202) 362-8566

Adorable clothing, toys and books for tots with a very friendly staff.

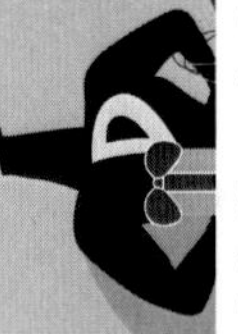

KRON CHOCOLATIER

Chevy Chase/Friendship Heights

5300 Wisconsin Ave. NW
Washington, DC 20015
(202) 966-4946 | www.krondc.com

Who can resist a tiny chocolate rotary phone? Also find delicious back-to-school and "camper care" packages. So beautiful they risk going uneaten. (Allowing that is not recommended!)

PERIWINKLE
Chevy Chase/Friendship Heights

3815 Livingston St. NW
Washington, DC 20015
(202) 364-3076

Great trinket, craft, and toy store with a wide candy selection in the back.

RAMER'S STRIDE RITE FOR KIDS
Chevy Chase/Friendship Heights

3810 N Hampton St. NW
Washington, DC 20015
(202) 244-2288 | www.striderite.com

Totally dedicated to cool kicks for kids! The place to get your kid stepping in style, or for that 4th pair of shoes this year for your growing boy.

BUSBOYS & POETS
Chinatown/Penn Quarter

1025 5th St. NW
Washington, DC 20001
(202) 789-2227 | www.busboysandpoets.com

Artsy and eclectic café and bookstore. Get the kids a cocoa and bring a coloring book, and you may have some time to sit for minute.

COP SHOP AT THE NATIONAL MUSEUM OF CRIME & PUNISHMENT
Chinatown/Penn Quarter

575 7th St. NW
Washington, DC 20004
(202) 621-5567

Fun merchandise for future crime fighters including retro vision glasses and very official-looking crime scene tape.

THE LIBRARY STORE
Chinatown/Penn Quarter

Martin Luther King Jr. Memorial Library
901 G St. NW
Washington, DC 20001
(202) 727-1205 | www.dclibrary.org

Shop for a cause before or after one of the library's cool events! Proceeds from the sale of posters, books, and small gifts are used to buy new books and materials for the Martin Luther King Jr. Memorial Library.

SPY STORE AT THE INTERNATIONAL SPY MUSEUM

Chinatown/Penn Quarter

800 F St. NW
Washington, District of Columbia 20004
(202) 393-7798 | www.spymuseum.org

WonderDads will be the coolest with a Jack-Bauer messenger bag. Kids will love the soda can safes for all their secret treasures. Plenty of neat books on the history of espionage and spy gizmos make for great nights under the covers with a flashlight reading!

DALTON BRODY LTD

Cleveland Park/Tenleytown/Van Ness

3412 Idaho Ave. NW
Washington, DC 20016
(202) 244-7197

Beautiful baby gifts featuring a wide silver selection. Also check out the darling apparel and chic diaper bags.

POLITICS AND PROSE

Cleveland Park/Tenleytown/Van Ness

5015 Connecticut Ave. NW
Washington, DC 20008
202-364-1919 or 800-722-0790 | www.politics-prose.com

Famous and well-loved independent bookstore. Politics and Prose has a fantastic selection of children's books and frequently hosts children's events including story times and author visits. Check the website for an events calendar. There are several each week!

SULLIVAN'S TOYS AND ART SUPPLIES

Cleveland Park/Tenleytown/Van Ness

3412 Wisconsin Ave. NW
Washington, DC 20016

You can find all the favorite toys and plenty of supplies for making crafts on a rainy day here! Great selection, Dads may even find something he wants!

TEMPO BOOK STORE

Cleveland Park/Tenleytown/Van Ness

4905 Wisconsin Ave. NW
Washington, DC 20016
(202) 363-6683 | www.tempobookdistributors.com

Plenty of resources for learning foreign languages—even for little ones!

WAKE-UP LITTLE SUZIE'S

Cleveland Park/Tenleytown/Van Ness

3409 Connecticut Ave. NW
Washington, DC 20008
202) 244-0700 | www.wakeuplittlesuzie.com

Lots of exciting things for everyone! Great baby gifts, neat toys, and handmade crafts. Check out a Secret Message-Writing Set!

GREATER GOODS

Columbia Heights/U Street

1626 U St. NW
Washington, DC 20009
(202) 449-6070 | greatergoods.com

A green and modern hybrid between a hardware and a homeware store. Greater Goods offers family-friendly workshops on how to "green" your home.

HOME RULE

Columbia Heights/U Street

1807 14th St. NW
Washington, DC 20009
(202) 797-5544 | homerule.com

A bountiful selection of funky toy robots live at this hip multi-colored Columbia Heights boutique. Also pick up some kooky kiddie flatware.

PULP DC

Columbia Heights/U Street

1803 14th St. NW
Washington, DC 20009
(202) 462-7857 | pulpdc.com

Cool gifts, toys, and novelties. Huge travel-themed section with fun maps of major world cities.

JUNCTION

Columbia Heights/U Street

1510 U St. NW
Washington, DC 20009
(202) 483-0261 | www.junctionwdc.com

You will feel like you're inside a dollhouse for people in this cute, cheery, and colorful vintage shop featuring children's clothes, funky accessories, and home furnishings.

BARNES AND NOBLE

Downtown

555 12th St. NW
Washington, DC 20004
(202) 347-0176 | www.barnesandnoble.com

Downtown DC's largest bookstore. You and the kids could spend hours exploring this place before you notice where the time's gone.

BORDERS BOOKS, MUSIC, MOVIES, AND CAFÉ

Downtown

1800 L St. NW
Washington, DC 20001
(202) 466-4999

Another great large bookstore with a large selection. Have the kids pick their own children's book to read together later.

CHOCOLATE CHOCOLATE

Downtown

1130 Connecticut Ave. NW
Washington, DC 20036
(202) 466-2190 | www.chocolatedc.com

So good it has to be said twice! Check out a chocolate Jefferson Memorial, chocolate Capitol Dome, or any of your other favorite monuments!

CHOCOLATE MOOSE

Downtown

1743 L St. NW
Washington, DC 20036
(202) 463-0992 | chocolatemoosedc.com

This family business has been owned by two sisters since 1978. The funky, whimsical, (and sometimes ridiculous) merchandise is always changing and includes candy, toys, baby accessories, home décor, jewelry, and more. A bountiful selection of wind-ups will entertain kids and dads alike!

PAT-A-CAKES

Downtown

Varying locations by event
Washington, DC
(202) 237-7389 | www.mypatacakes.com

Create life long memories with custom ceramic impressions of little hands and feet. Customizable colors and styles. Call for a personal appointment, view the website for upcoming events, or organize all the other WonderDads and their kids, and get your own kid's pat-a-cake for free.

UTRECHT

Downtown

1250 I St. NW
Washington, DC 20005-3922
(202) 898-0555 | www.utrecht.com

The artist staff knows their stuff. The place is huge and has anything for any type of craft you or your little ones can imagine!

WHITE HOUSE GIFT SHOP

Downtown

529 14th St. NW #807
Washington, DC 20045-1801
(202) 662-7280 | whitehousegiftshop.com

The official gift shop of the White House. Pick up a model kit and build your own mini White House together!

BIAGO FINE CHOCOLATE

DuPont

1904 18th St. NW
Washington, DC 20009
(202) 328-1506 | www.biagiochocolate.com

Chocolates from all over the world! Everywhere from Arlington to Madagascar! All offerings are fair-trade. The staff is happy to educate on the chocolate-making process.

BOOKS-A-MILLION

DuPont

11 Dupont Circle NW
Washington, DC 20036
(202) 319-1374 | booksamillion.com

Huge selection and awesome location right on DuPont Circle.

BOOKS FOR AMERICA

DuPont

1417 22nd St. NW
Washington, DC 20037
(202) 835.2665 | www.booksforamerica.org

This nonprofit collects books for donation and also has its own bookstore in DuPont. The staff can also help you set up and plan your own book drive.

GINZA

DuPont

1721 Connecticut Ave. NW
Washington, DC 20009
(202) 332-7000 | www.ginzaonline.com

Ample offering of Japanese folding paper that is perfect for making origami on a rainy day.

KIDS CLOSET DC

DuPont

1226 Connecticut Ave. NW
Washington D.C., DC 20036
(202) 429-9247 | www.kidsclosetdc.com

Unique kids clothes and toys in DC. Also carrying the most popular brands including Lego, Carter, and I Play.

KRAMER BOOKS AND AFTERWORDS CAFÉ

DuPont

1517 Connecticut Ave. NW
Washington, DC 20036
(202) 387-1462 | www.kramers.com

Bookstore and café in one! A great place to spend a wet or snowy afternoon.

RED ONION RECORDS AND BOOKS

DuPont

1901 18th St. NW
Washington, DC 20009
(202) 986-2718 | redonionrecordsandbooks.com

Plenty of neat graphic novels and old vinyl at this rock-orientated store.

SECOND STORY BOOKS

DuPont

2000 P St. NW
Washington, DC 20036
(202) 659-8884 | secondstorybooks.com

DC's premiere used book store. Second Story also has a cool assortment of vintage posters and other antiques.

TABLETOP

DuPont

1608 20th St. NW
Washington, DC 20009
(202) 387-7117 | www.tabletopdc.com

Cool knickknacks and home décor that will look cool in any kids' hangout.

APPLE STORE

Georgetown

1229 Wisconsin Ave. NW
Washington, DC 20007
(202) 572-1460 | www.apple.com

There is a table set up with plenty of kid-height Macs loaded with games for kids to play while parents peruse.

BARNES AND NOBLE

Georgetown

3040 M St. NW
Washington, DC 20007
(202) 965-9880 | www.barnesandnoble.com

Classic big-box bookstore has everything coupled with outstanding hours.

BARTLEBY'S BOOKS

Georgetown

3034 M St. NW
Washington, DC 20007
(202) 298-0486

Rare and antique books with a focus on American history.

BIG PLANET COMICS

Georgetown

Georgetown 3145 Dumbarton St.
NW Washington, DC 20007
(202) 342-1961 | www.bigplanetcomics.com

Offers independent and alternative hip comics. Special section devoted to children's comics.

BRIDGE STREET BOOKS

Georgetown

2814 Pennsylvania Ave. NW
Washington, DC
(202) 965-5200

Small and quirky independent bookstore. A great place to find the off-beat parenting book or memoir that puts it all in perspective.

DAWN PRICE BABY

Georgetown

3112 M St. NW
Washington, DC 20007
(202) 333-3939 | www.dawpricebaby.com

Super knowledgeable and friendly sales staff knows their stuff on all products baby. They have it all at this beautiful boutique: toys, trinkets, onesies, strollers, and high chairs. Great place to get an outfit for a special occasion.

GODIVA CHOCOLATIER

Georgetown

3242 M St. NW
Washington, DC 20007
(202) 333-5864 | www.godiva.com

The alpha and omega of chocolate has an outpost in the heart of Georgetown.

J. CHOCOLATIER

Georgetown

1039 33rd St. NW
Washington, DC 20007
(202) 333-4111 | www.jchocolatier.com

Goat cheese truffles must not go uninvestigated! Dozens of varietes of truffles with a daily rotating menu. Do shots (of lavender vanilla bean cocoa) with the kids.

JUICY COUTURE

Georgetown

3034 M St.
Washington, DC 20007
www.juicycouture.com

Darling outfits and lounge wear for all the hippest little girls in DC.

LOST BOYS

Georgetown

1033 31st St. NW
(at N Waters Ally)
Washington, DC 20007
(202) 333-0093 | www.lostboysdc.com

This trendy men's boutique with its helpful staff can get WonderDads on the fast track to chic. No fanny packs in here!

LULULEMON ATHLETICA

Georgetown

3265 M St. NW
Washington, DC 20007
(202) 333-1738 | www.lululemon.com

High quality workout gear for WonderDads. Great bags that go from gym to work to schlepping kids around.

LUSH

Georgetown

3066 M St. NW
Washington, DC 20007
(202) 333-6950 | www.lush.com

The smell alone will be enough to lure you into this soap and body product shop. Kids will love picking out their own bath-time potions amongst all the smells, bright colors and textures.

MORGAN'S SWEET CLUB

Georgetown

www.morganssweetclub.com

Dessert catering service especially for children. They will cater whatever your little one can imagine or bring the implements to host a "decorate your own" party. Fantastic for birthdays!

NIDO

Georgetown

1425 Wisconsin Ave. NW
Washington, DC 20007
(202) 333-5445 | www.nidodc.com

Plenty of unique kids items and accessories.

PAPER SOURCE

Georgetown

(301) M St. NW
Washington, DC 20007
(202) 298-5545 | www.paper-source.com

This stationary store has all you need to make your own scrapbook, photo album, or calendar.

PATAGONIA

Georgetown

1048 Wisconsin Ave. NW
Washington, DC 20007
(202) 333-1776 | www.patagonia.com

Great outdoor gear for the whole family including your little vagabond. Also plenty of gear for climbing, hiking, and skiing.

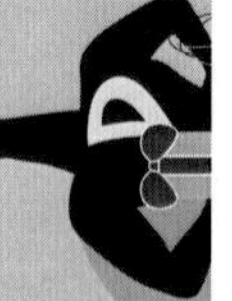

PICCOLO PIGGIES

Georgetown

1533 Wisconsin Ave. NW
Washington, DC 20007
(202) 333-0123 | www.piccolo-piggies.com

The cutest kids clothes in town including mini-me sized Lilly Pultizer and Ralph Lauren. All ages from baby to ten. The second floor is dedicated to party dresses. Cool dad-friendly diaper bags too!

PRESSE BOOKSTORE

Georgetown

1614 Wisconsin Ave. NW
Washington, DC 20007
(202) 338-1594 | www.pressebooks.com

A wide selection of beautiful and unqiue books books for children including many books written in French or to help teach French. Try out "Le Chat Chapeaute" (the Cat in the Hat en francais) or Yetta the Yiddish Chicken!

PROPER TOPPER

Georgetown

3213 P St. NW
Washington, DC 20007
(202) 333-6200 | www.propertopper.com

Plenty of baby gifts and clothing for babies and older children.

REVOLUTION CYCLES

Georgetown

3411 M St. NW
Washington, DC 20007
(202) 965-3601 | www.revolutioncycles.com

This cycle shop takes the time to fit you or your little ones perfectly to a bike. One year of free adjustments is included in the price. Massive amount of bike accessories too!

SASSANOVA

Georgetown

1641 Wisconsin Ave. NW
Washington, DC 20050
(202) 471-4400 | www.sassanova.com

Headbands and an entire wall of various hair bows and barettes. Plenty of cute mini shoes for little girls.

TUGOOH TOYS

Georgetown

1319 Wisconsin Ave. NW
Washington, DC 20007
(202) 338-9476 | www.yirostores.com

All natural, eco-friendly, educational toys. The famed Ugly Dolls have a big outpost here.

TWIXT
Georgetown

3319A Cadys Alley NW
Washington, DC 20007
(202) 333-3274 | shoptwixt.com

Your little princess will be the chicest girl on the block with the selections from this super cool boutique.

URBAN CHIC
Georgetown

1626 Wisconsin Ave. NW
Washington, DC 20007
(202) 338-5398 | www.urbanchiconline.com

Chic looks for kids and adults from up and coming designers and old favorites alike!

VINEYARD VINES
Georgetown

1225 Wisconsin Ave. NW
Washington, DC 20007
(202) 625-8463 | www.vineyardvines.com

Large children's selection makes matching daddy and me prepster outfits a very likely possibility.

YIRO
Georgetown

1419 Wisconsin Ave. NW
Washington, DC 20007
(202) 333-0032 | www.yirostores.com

Sister store to Tugooh Toys also offering eco-friendly toys, games, and clothing. A great place to find the birthday gift for the little lefty on your list.

AGAPE BEARS
Logan Circle

4238 Wilson Blvd Ste 2170
Arlington, VA 22203
(703) 841-2444 | www.agapebears.com

All teddy bears, all the time. But plenty of other animals too!

MISS PIXIE'S
Logan Circle

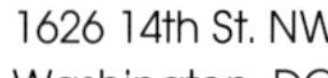

1626 14th St. NW
Washington, DC 20009
(202) 232-8171 | www.misspixies.com

Miss Pixie's carries "furnishings and whatnot!" Some of the whimsical whatnot includes vintage dolls, games, and other toys.

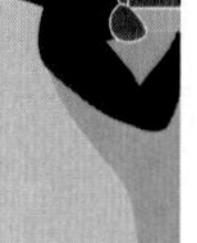

MONARCH CARNIVAL SUPPLY COMPANY

Logan Circle

1331 14th St. NW
Washington, DC 20005
(202) 462-5533

The weirdest store in D.C! Monarch carries any and all novelties imaginable. Giant stuffed animals, inflatable hammers, and other campy carnival curiousities.

APPLE SEED BOUTIQUE

NoVa

115 S Columbus St.
Alexandria, VA
(703) 535-5446 | Appleseedboutique.com

Trendy maternity and cute infant clothing including hilarious play-on-words onseis. Appleseed also features Bugaboo strollers, and a variety of baby and new mom gifts.

BIG PLANET COMICS

NoVa

426 Maple Ave. E
Vienna, VA 22180
(703) 242-9412 | www.bigplanetcomics.com

Offers independent and alternative hip comics. Special section devoted to children's comics.

CARTOON CUTS

NoVa

11784-U Fair Oaks Mall
Fairfax , VA 22033
703-359-2887

This fun and funky environment caters to kids' hairstyling needs. They have Family Plans that include one child and one adult haircut at discount prices. Bring all the kids at once, save bundle, and get a trim for yourself at the same time.

DOODLEHOPPER FOR KIDS

NoVa

28 W Broad St.
Falls Church, VA 22046
(703) 241-2262 | www.hunstmandoodlehopper.com

Educational toys, unique gifts, plenty of clothes and costumes. Special "Girl Power" and "Boys Rule" sections.

ECLIPSE KIDS

NoVa

1373 Beverly Rd.
McLean, VA 22101
(703) 356-0064

Completely child-friendly environment. Miss Irma is great with little girls! The salon caters to adults as well, so the family can beautify in one stop!

STORES

ISPARITO

NoVa

2620 Wilson Blvd
Arlington, VA 22201
(703) 875-8182

Modern interior design emphasizing color and simple shapes—perfect finds for kids' rooms!

KINDER HAUS CLOTHES

NoVa

1220 N. Fillmore St.
Arlington, VA 22201
(703) 527-5929 | www.kinderhaus.com

"Toys powered by imagination, not batteries." Old-fashioned toy store offering books, toys, clothing, shoes, and crafts. Don't miss the adorable Folkmanis Puppets!

THE LITTLE MONOGRAM SHOP

NoVa

106 N Columbus St.
Alexandria, VA 22314
(703) 549-3777

Get your junior prepster started young. Personalized tote bags, blankets, onesies, bibs, sippy cups — anything you can think of. Plus, they will monogram anything you bring in.

ONE TWO KANGAROO TOYS

NoVa

4022 28th St. S
Arlington, VA 22206
(703) 845-9099

The top sellers in each brand and all the old-school favorites too!

PURPLE GOOSE

NoVa

2005 Mt. Vernon Ave
Alexandria, VA 22301
(703) 683-2918 | www.thepurplegoose.com

Little girls will be in heaven amidst the whirl of dress up clothes, whimsical outfits, darling jewelry, dolls, play kitchens and more!

SCHAKOLAD CHOCOLATE FACTORY

NoVa

2461 S Clark St.
Arlington, VA 22202
(703) 418-2000

Try the chocolate dipped Oreos for an extra decadent special treat!

THE BEST DAD/CHILD OUTDOOR PARKS & RECREATION

KALORAMA PARK

Adams Morgan

19th St. NW and Kalorama Rd.
(202) 673-7606 | www.kaloramapark.com

The playground at this park is divided into special areas for big kids and little kids. The rec center at the park hosts an awesome annual Halloween Party for little ones.

MARIE REED RECREATION CENTER AND HAPPY HALLOW CHILDREN'S POOL

Adams Morgan

2200 Champlain St. NW
Washington, DC 20050
(202) 673-7771 | www.dpr.dc.gov

Lighted outdoor basketball courts and free public pool. Kickboard and floats are available for use.

MITCHELL PARK

Adams Morgan

23rd St. and S St.
Washington, DC 20008
www.dpr.dc.gov

A tot lot and a beautiful fenced-in garden.

BELLE ZIEGLER PARK

Bethesda & Maryland

Takoma Ave. and Albany Ave.
Takoma Park, MD 20912
www.tprecreation.org

A kid-friendly half-basketballl court and t-ball field.

FOREST PARK

Bethesda & Maryland

Prince Georges Ave. and Elm Ave.
Takoma Park, MD 20912
www.tprecreation.org

Playground, two half basketballs courts, and a teeball field.

GLEN ECHO PARK

Bethesda & Maryland

7300 MacArthur Blvd.
Glen Echo, MD 20812
(301) 634-2222 | www.glenechopark.org

Glen Echo Park is a magical place on the Potomac Palisades! The park is abound with fun activities for kids. There are playgroups, a puppet theatre, music, dance, and writing classes and much more! A romp in the playground is always fun and so is a ride on the fabulous Dentzel Carousel! There are always plenty of fun events. Check the website for details.

HEFFNER PARK

Bethesda & Maryland

42 Oswego Ave.
Takoma Park, MD 20912
www.tprecreation.org

Playground with a half basketball court. Give your kid a lift and have him dunk!

SPRING PARK

Bethesda & Maryland

Elm Ave. and Poplar Ave.
Takoma Park, MD 20912
www.tprecreation.org

Teeball fields, a spring, and a playground make this a great neighborhood retreat.

ANACOSTIA PARK

Capitol Hill/Northeast/Southeast

1900 Anacostia Dr. SE
Washington, DC 20020

At over 1200 acres, Anacostia Park is one of D.C.'s largest recreation areas. Kenilworth Park, Kenilworth Marsh, and the Aquatic Garden offer beautiful natural exhibits. There is an 18-hole public golf course and driving range as well.

FOLGER PARK

Capitol Hill/Northeast/Southeast

3rd & D Sts. SE
Washington, DC 20003

This is one of the largest parks in the Capitol Hill area. This park is home to over one thousand ornamental trees!

FORT DUPONT PARK

Capitol Hill/Northeast/Southeast

Fort Davis Dr. and Massachusetts Ave. SE
Washington, DC 20019
www.nps.gov/fodu

Fort DuPont Park is one of the forts that are collectively known as the Civil War Defenses of Washington. This park is home to the only public indoor ice skating rink in D.C. Plenty of Civil War educational events. Fort DuPont is also home to the ever-popular Fort DuPont Summer Concert Series. Obtaining a plot in the Fort DuPont Community Gardens can make for a great family activity.

GARFIELD PARK

Capitol Hill/Northeast/Southeast

3rd & G Sts. SE
Washington, DC 20003
www.dpr.dc.gov

Fun, oversized playground equipment that WonderDads can play on too!

LANGSTON RECREATIONAL CENTER AND GOLF COURSE

Capitol Hill/Northeast/Southeast

24th and H St. NE
Washington, DC 20019
(202) 472-3884

Very inexpensive and un-crowded, Langston Golf Course is great for just-beginning junior golfers. Check out the Langston Grill for a bite too. The nearby playground is fun for afterwards!

LINCOLN CAPPER CHILDREN'S POOL

Capitol Hill/Northeast/Southeast

500 L St. SE
Washington, DC 20001
(202) 727-1080 | www.dpr.dc.gov

A brand new pool that opened just this year! Rock your board shorts with the little ones in tow, and teach them to kick and paddle in a safe and fun new place.

LINCOLN PARK

Capitol Hill/Northeast/Southeast

East Capitol and 11th Sts. NE
Washington, DC 20002

Located directly east of the U.S. Capitol, this park is a perfect restful pitstop after a tour. The park also hosts many special commemorative ceremonies.

LOVEJOY PARK

Capitol Hill/Northeast/Southeast

12th & E St.s NE
Washington, DC 20002
www.dpr.dc.gov

Lovejoy Park has a small, well cared-for playground and plenty of room to run around and toss a ball!

MARION PARK

Capitol Hill/Northeast/Southeast

E St. and South Carolina Ave. NE
Washington, DC 20003

This park was included in the original city plan from 1791. There is a toddler-friendly play area in one quadrant of the park.

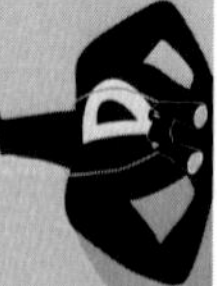

NATIONAL ARBORETUM

Capitol Hill/Northeast/Southeast

3501 New York Ave. NE
Washington, DC 20002
www.usna.usda.gov

The Arboretum's biggest draw is the National Bonsai and Peijing Museum, which features over 150 miniature trees. There is also a koi pond and a rock garden. Twenty-two Corinthian columns planted in a grassy filed near the entrance were originally part of the Capitol Building. An open-air passenger train runs through the Arboretum on a 35 minute narrated tour.

STANTON PARK

Capitol Hill/Northeast/Southeast

C St. and 4th St. NE
Washington, DC 20002

Stanton park is a wonderful example of the natural and urban aesthetic in the design of the Nation's Capitol. There is a play area located west of the General Nathanel Greene statue.

TURKEY THICKET RECREATION CENTER

Capitol Hill/Northeast/Southeast

1100 Michigan Ave. NE
Washington, DC 20017
(202) 576-9238 | wwww.dpr.dc.gov

Newly-renovated and a special pool just for kids. There are also basketball and tennis courts and a playground.

CLEVELAND PARK CLUB

Cleveland Park/Tenleytown/Van Ness

3433 33rd Pl NW
Washington, DC 20008
www.clevelandparkclub.org

A heated pool and swim lessons offered for kids of all ages. A camp runs every summer and offers a variety of fun activities to fill hot days!

FORT RENO PARK

Cleveland Park/Tenleytown/Van Ness

3800 Donaldson Pl NW
Washington, DC 20018

Notorious for fun summer concerts featuring local musicians. Bring a blanket and some take out and enjoy!

MARVIN GAYE REC CENTER (WATTS BRANCH PARK)

Cleveland Park/Tenleytown/Van Ness

6201 Banks Pl. NE
Washington, DC 200019
(202) 727-7432 | www.dpr.dc.gov

Go check out "Watts" going on! Marvin Gaye started his musical life not far from this park. The rec center is closed on Sundays.

MELVIN C. HAZEN PARK

Cleveland Park/Tenleytown/Van Ness

Rodman St. NW and Connecticut Ave. NW
Washington, DC 20008

A quiet, smaller, park with a trail that leads to larger Rock Creek Park.

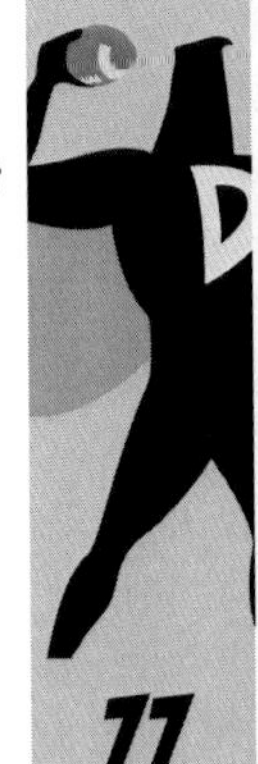

KENNEDY PLAYGROUND AND RECREATION CENTER

Columbia Heights/U Street

1401 7th St. NW
Washington, DC 20001
(202) 671-4792 | www.dpr.dc.gov

Amenities at the Kennedy Recreation Center include two lit basketball courts, a baseball field, two playgrounds (one for little kids, one for bigger kids), a tennis court, picnic areas, and a multi-purpose room and computer room. The center also offers a variety of classes.

MERIDIAN HILL MALCOLM X PARK

Columbia Heights/U Street

16th St. NW
Washington, DC 20009
www.nps.gov/mehi

Originally home to Columbia College, precursor to George Washington University. Prior to the Civil War, the mansion grounds became a pleasure park for the area. During the war, Union troops encamped there. Meridian Hill Park was designated a National Historic Landmark in 1994, as "an outstanding accomplishment of early 20th-century Neoclassicist park design in the United States." Stop by on Sunday and see the drummers perform. Each week, a few dozen folks bring drums of all kinds and jam in a circle.

PARKVIEW CHILDREN'S POOL

Columbia Heights/U Street

693 Otis Pl. NW
Washington, DC 20010
(202) 576-5750 | www.dpr.dc.gov

Children six and under swim free! Children 6-13 are only $3 per visit.

BATTERY KEMBLE PARK

Downtown

Chain Bridge Rd. and Macarthur Blvd. NW
Washington, DC 20016
www.nps.gov/cwdw/historyculture/battery-kemble.htm

During the Civil War, the site held a battery to the Chain Bridge. A 57 acre park was established around the historic site. Plenty of scenic walking trails!

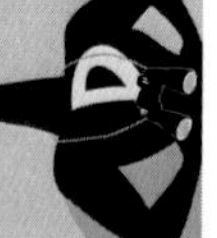

CONSTITUTION GARDENS

Downtown

Constitution Ave. and 17th St. NW
Washington, DC 20006
www.nps.gov/coga

A memorial island in the middle of a man-made lake features stones bearing the names and signatures of the fifty-six men who signed the Declaration of Independence. Check out the Reflecting Pool and the Lincoln Memorial, too.

FRANCIS POOL

Downtown

2435 N St. NW
Washington, DC 20037
(202) 727-3285 | www.drp.dc.gov

Three pools here! One is a separate, smaller pool for little kids and babies. Lots of room to spread out! Free for DC residents.

PERSHING PARK

Downtown

14th St. NW & Pennsylvania Ave.
Washington, DC 20004
www.nps.gov

Feed the downtown ducks at the pond in this park! Perfect for a stop before or after touring monuments or museums. In the winter, the pond is turned into an ice rink.

PRESIDENT'S PARK

Downtown

1600 Pennsylvania Ave.
Washington, DC 20004
www.nps.gov/whho

The first family lives in a national park! The White House and President's Park, have been a part of the national park system since 1933. President's Park is the park land surrounding the White House and its grounds. It includes the Ellipse, Lafayette Park, Sherman Park and the 1st Division Monument. Activities in President's Park include interpretive presentations and walks, junior ranger programs, special events, and guided tours.

SONNY BONO PARK

DuPont Circle

New Hampshire Ave. 20th St. and O St.
Washington, DC 20036

Yes, this is for real! A tiny little triangle of grass is perfect for a little rest after milling around DuPont. A large plaque commemorates the entertainer-gone-statesman.

FRIENDSHIP "TURTLE" PARK

Friendship Heights

4500 Van Ness St. NW
Washington, DC 20016
(202) 282-2198 | www.turtlepark.org

One of the most well-loved playgrounds in D.C. This park has plenty of slides, tunnels, sandboxes, and swings. There are also basketball and tennis courts along with soccer fields. For chilling out after, there is a fenced in area with picnic tables. Turtle Park also operates a pre-school for children ages 2 ½ to 5. Don't miss the spray park in the summer!

OUTDOOR PARKS

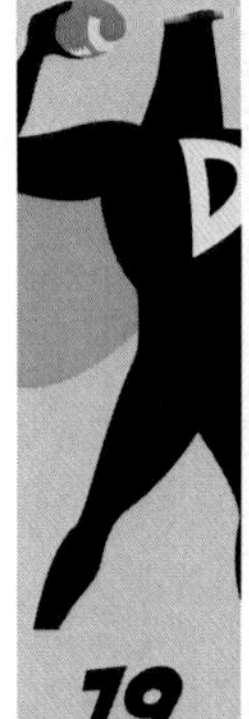

FORT BAYARD PARK

Friendship Heights

Western Ave. and 46th St. NW
www.dpr.dc.gov

The park once was home to a Civil War fort. Features a spruced-up playground.

LAFEYETTE RECREATION CENTER AND SPRAY PARK

Friendship Heights

33rd St. NW & Patterson St. NW
Washington, DC 20015
(202) 282-2206 | www.dpr.dc.gov

A picnic area, playground, tennis and basketball courts, plus a small spray park to cool off hot kids on a sweltering DC summer day.

BOOK HILL PARK

Georgetown

1693 Wisconsin Ave. NW
(between N R St. & N Reservoir Rd)
Washington, DC 20007

Need an escape from the hustle and bustle of Wisconsin Ave.? Tiny pristine park located directly behind the Georgetown Library. Check out some books then read together on the park's benches.

CHESAPEAKE AND OHIO NATIONAL HISTORIC PARK

Georgetown

1057 Thomas Jefferson St. NW
Washington, DC 20007
202-653-5190 | www.nps.gov/choh

Preserving America's colorful Canal era and transportation history, the Chesapeake & Ohio Canal National Historical Park is miles of adventure!

DUMBARTON OAKS PARK

Georgetown

31st and R St. NW
Washington, DC 20007
www.doaks.org

A pretty and quiet park with beautiful gardens.

FRANCIS SCOTT KEY PARK

34th & M St. NW
Washington, DC 20007

A tucked away gem with plenty of open green space for kicking around a soccer ball or tossing the Frisbee with Fido.

GEORGETOWN WATERFRONT PARK

Georgetown

3000 K St. NW
Washington, DC 20007
www.georgetownwaterfrontpark.org

Brand new! Plenty of waterfront car free pathways for strolling and bike ridng. Ample green space for picnicking. Perfect for after brunch or lunch at one of Georgetown's many kid-friendly restaurants.

MONTROSE PARK

Georgetown

32nd and R St. NW
Washington, DC 20007

A well-kept local secret! You will be unable to see another building or hear a single car inside this urban oasis. There is a playground with swings and a path that leads to nearby Dumbarton Oaks Park.

ROSE PARK

Georgetown

26th & O St. NW
Washington, DC 20007
(202) 282-2208

Two sand-surfaced playgrounds, basketball court, and a baseball diamond make this a perfect kids' reprieve. Lots of dogs here too.

VOLTA PARK

Georgetown

3400 Volta Pl.
(between N 34th St. & N 35th St.)
Washington, DC 20007
(202) 282-0381 | www.dpr.dc.gov

One of the best pubic pools in D.C. Come early for a chair! There are also tennis courts and beautiful magnolia trees to lounge under.

GLOVER ARCHBOLD PARK

Glover Park

42nd St. NW and Davis Pl. NW
Washington, DC 20007
www.dpr.dc.gov

Playground and plenty of green space to run around! A perfect stop before Stroller Happy Hour at Blue Ridge!

ROCK CREEK PARK

Glover Park

5200 Glover Rd. NW
Washington, DC 20015
www.nps.gov/rocr

Fresh air, majestic trees, wild animals, and the gurgle of Rock Creek make it the perfect city oasis. The Carter Barron Amphitheatre located inside the park hosts a variety of fun summer events. Stop by the nearby Planetarium too!

OUTDOOR PARKS

BARTHOLDI PARK

Southwest

Independence Ave. and 1st St. SW
Washington, DC 20024
www.usbg.gov/gardens/barthodli-park.cfm

Part of the U.S. Botanical Garden, this park is home to many beautiful flowers and a fountain designed by a sculptor who assisted with the Statue of Liberty!

EAST POTOMAC PARK-HAINES POINT

Southwest

Ohio Dr. SW
Washington, DC 20024
www.nps.gov/state/dc

Miniature golf, swimming pools, tennis courts, golf course with driving range and plenty of bike and walking trails. This park is also home to D.C.'s famous Cherry Trees!

RANDALL RECREATION CENTER

Southwest

820 S Capitol St. SW
Washington, DC 20001
(202) 727-5504 | www.dpr.dc.gov

Facilities include a huge pool, lighted athletics fields, tennis and basketball courts along with a well-equipped playground and arts and crafts room.

WEST POTOMAC PARK

Southwest

Independence Ave. SW
Washington, DC 20418
www.nps.gov/state/dc

West Potomac Park is adjacent to the National Mall and west of the Washington Monument. The park is home to many national memorials including World War II, Vietnam and Korean Wars, and Presidents Lincoln, Jefferson, and FDR.

ALCOVA HEIGHTS PARK

NoVa

901 S. George Mason Dr.
Arlington, VA 22204
www.arlingtonva.us

This park boasts a newly renovated playground, volleyball courts, a youth only baseball diamond, picnic tables and grills!

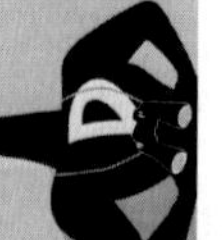

BENJAMIN BANNEKER PARK

NoVa

1701 N Van Buren St.
Arlington, VA 22205
www.arlingtonva.us

A circular park with a beautiful view of the Potomac River. A nice place to rest at the end of the L'Enfant Promenade.

BLUEMONT PARK

NoVa

601 N Manchester St.
Arlington, VA 22203
www.arlingtonva.us

Huge park (over 70 acres!) includes several playgrounds, a Frisbee golf course and three youth-only baseball diamonds.

BON AIR PARK AND MEMORIAL ROSE GARDEN

NoVa

850 N Lexington St.
Arlington, VA 22205
www.arlingtonva.us

Come and enjoy the beautiful flowers, ornamental tree gardens, playgrounds, sports courts, and picnic areas.

CAMERON RUN REGIONAL PARK

NoVa

4001 Eisenhower Ave.
Alexandria, VA 22304
(703) 960-0767 | www.nrvpa.org

Cameron Run Regional Park offers a variety of recreation facilities including Great Waves Water Park, miniature golf, batting cages, and picnic shelters.

DREW PARK

NoVa

3514 22nd St. S
Arlington, VA 22204
www.arlingtonva.us

A brand new playground features some unique pieces! There is also a spray park open in the summer! The park sits at the bottom of a fun steep slope, great for running up and rolling down.

FORT C.F. SMITH PARK

NoVa

11 N 24th St.
Arlington VA 22207
www.arlingtonva.us

This beautiful 19-acre site includes, an open meadow, the lovely restored 20th century mansion, Hendry House, and preserved ruins of a Civil War fort built in 1863. A man-made bird creek attracts migrating birds. Expect to see Scarlet Tanagers, Baltimore Orioles, Eastern Meadowlarks, Common Yellowthroats and more!

THEODORE ROOSEVELT ISLAND

NoVa

George Washington Memorial Pkwy.
Arlington, VA 22216
www.nps.gov/this

Theodore Roosevelt Island is accessible only from the northbound lanes of the George Washington Memorial Parkway. The entrance to the parking lot is located just north of the Roosevelt Bridge. The Island has several trails and a boardwalk that allows you to view wildlife in the forest and swamp. Also learn about President Roosevelt's legacy while viewing the Memorial Plaza.

GRAVELLY POINT PARK

NoVa

George Washington Memorial Pkwy.
Arlington, VA 22202

Pack a picnic lunch and watch planes land and take off from nearby Ronald Reagan airport. There are always plenty of families fishing, boating, and cycling. There is a lot to see so bring a camera! You can see the airport in one direction, the U.S. Capitol Building in another, and the Washington Monument and Jefferson memorial in another. If you are a fan of lights, go at night. The runway and airport lights are surprisingly spectacular.

GREAT FALLS PARK

NoVa

9200 Old Dominion Rd.
McLean, VA 22101
703-285-2965 | www.nps.gov/gwmp/gfra

Come see where the Potomac River cascades into 20-foot waterfalls. Picnic tables and grills are available on a first-come, first-served basis. Hike the trails or bird-watch, fish, or horseback ride.

HAYES PARK

NoVa

1516 N. Lincoln St.
Arlington, VA 22201
www.arlingtonva.us

This small park is perfect for small people! There are two playgrounds and the spray park operates in the summertime.

JEFFERSON DISTRICT PARK

NoVa

900 Lee Hwy.
Falls Church, VA 22042
(703) 573-0444 | www.fairfaxcounty.gov

Go for the miniature golf, stay and lounge for a picnic after.

LACEY WOODS PARK

NoVa

1200 N George Mason Dr.
Arlington, VA 22205
www.arlingtonva.us

Picnic tables with shelter, charcoal grills, nature trails, gardens, and a playground with top-notch equipment including tunnels and crawl bridges make this a perfect spot to pass the afternoon.

LUBBER RUN PARK

NoVa

300 N Park Dr.
Arlington, VA 22203
www.arlingtonva.us

Two playgrounds, picnic area with grills, and multiple sport courts. An amphitheatre hosts fun summer performances.

QUINCY PARK

NoVa

1021 N Quincy St.
Arlington, VA 22216
www.arlingtonva.us

Tennis courts, a softball field, basketball courts and a picnic area with pavilion.

UPTON HILL REGIONAL PARK

NoVa

6060 Wilson Blvd.
Arlington, VA 22205
(703) 534-3437 | www.nvrpa.org

A large outdoor water park complex is a sparkling attraction in this wooded, urban park. The water park features slides, a spray park, a kiddie pool and more! There is also a miniature golf course.

VIRGINIA HIGHLANDS PARK

NoVa

1600 S Hayes St.
Arlington, VA 22202

Very family friendly and plenty of open space for kids to run around! Two playgrounds, basketball courts, baseball diamonds, picnic tables, and charcoal grills make it an excellent spot for a family afternoon! There is also a public library nearby.

WINDY RUN PARK

NoVa

2420 N Kenmore St.
Arlington, VA 22207
www.arlingtonva.us

Stroll along the many trails and frolic in this wide-open space.

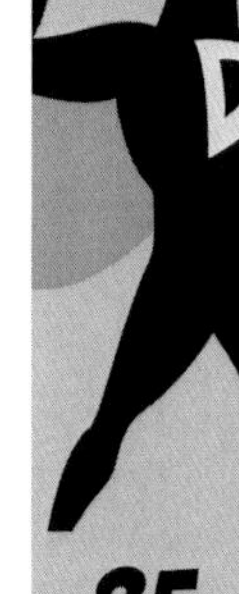

CAPITAL CRESCENT TRAIL

www.cctrail.org

Built upon the abandoned railbed of the 11 mile Georgetown Branch of the B&O Railroad. This trail goes from Georgetown to Silver Spring, M.D. Perfect for a walk or bike ride!

CAPTAIN JOHN SMITH CHESAPEAKE NATIONAL HISTORIC TRAIL

www.smithtrail.net

Follow in the wake of Captain Smith's adventures nearly 400 years ago on the Captain John Smith Historic Trail.

MOUNT VERNON TRAIL

www.nps.gov

A great option to feel far out of the city without having to go a great distance! The trail is very well-maintained and mostly flat making it perfect for strollers and little ones.

POTOMAC HERITAGE NATIONAL SCENIC TRAIL

www.nps.gov/pohe

The Potomac Heritage National Scenic Trail is a network of locally-managed trails between the mouth of the Potomac River and the Allegheny Highlands.

STAR SPANGLED BANNER NATIONAL HISTORIC TRAIL

www.nps.gov/stsp

This trail tells the stories of the people, events, and places that led to the birth of our National Anthem. The trail is still being developed, but already has many open sites and landscapes.

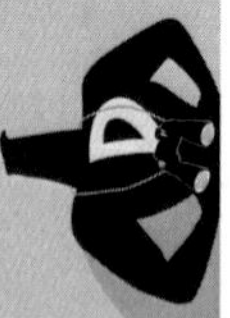

THE BEST DAD/CHILD UNIQUE ADVENTURES

ADVENTURE PARK USA

11113 W Baldwin Rd.
New Market MD 21774
301-865-6800 | www.adventureparkusa.com

Approximately one hour and ten minutes from downtown D.C.
FREE admission! Pick and choose your attractions and add credits to your pass. Go back to the Wild West at Adventure Park USA! Rollercoasters, a arcade, bumper boats, mini golf, go karts, playgrounds, laser tag, and a ropes course are just some of the attractions here. There is also a special area for smaller cowhands including a carousel, teacups, moon bounce, and a Create-a-Critter station. Come on a rainy day too! There is a four-story indoor play area. Adventure Park USA is more than just a family entertainment center. They also offer preschool, day care, summer camp, and a before and after school program.

ANNAPOLIS, MARYLAND

Approximately 45 minutes from downtown D.C.
Plenty to do for kids in this idyllic waterside city! The Chesapeake Children's Museum has a several interactive exhibits. You can try your hand at crabbing at Sandy Point Park. The city is full of gorgeous playgrounds. There is also a Six Flags Theme Park worthy of a trip in itself.

BALTIMORE, MARYLAND

Approximately one hour from downtown D.C.
There is plenty for WonderDads and kids to do in Baltimore! The Aquarium is amongst the best in the U.S. and has an astounding dolphin show. The zoo is also not to be missed. Stop to feed the giraffes—how fun are blue tongues?! The Maryland Science Center boasts a planetarium, IMAX theatre, and plenty of hands-on demonstrations for kids. The National Museum of Dentistry is a quirky surprise and has amazing collection of dental doohickeys, from George Washington's not-so-wooden denture to a cautionary "Mr. Gross Mouth." The Inner Harbor area has plenty of kid friendly shops and restaurants and is perfect for strolling.

BETHANY BEACH, DELAWARE

Approximately three hours from downtown D.C.
This quiet beach town is perfect for families. Bethany Beach has plenty of free beaches that are great for children of all ages. The coasts here are cleaner than most and lend themselves to all kinds of fun aquatic recreation such as kite-flying, boogie boarding, body surfing, and sandcastle-building. The bandstand features free family-friendly performances every evening in season. You'll see everything from brass bands, magicians, jugglers, folk musicians, kids' theatre groups, to animal acts. Often they'll call kids up to the stage as volunteers, so sit close!

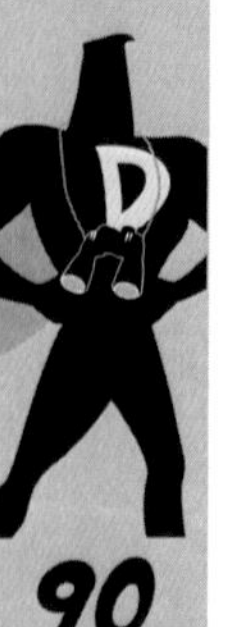

BROOKSIDE GARDENS

1800 Glenallan Ave. Wheaton, MD 20902

301-962-1400 or 301-962-1404 | www.montgomeryparks.org

Approximately 30 minutes from downtown D.C.

Beauty everywhere you turn! There are plenty of children's classes and events at this huge park. Face painting, story times, and craft activities, and scavenger hunts are always happening. Children are invited to "grown their own mini salad garden." Garden Tea Parties are hosted often and make for a fanciful afternoon of tea and treats. Children will learn proper tea etiquette, socialize, and play flamingo croquet weather permitting. The "Wings of Fancy" butterfly exhibit is a must for sunny days (butterflies are most active in bright light!) The South Conservatory is closed Sept. 20- Oct. 9 and the North Conservatory is closed Sept. 27- Oct. 9.

BUTLER'S ORCHARD

22200 Davis Mill Rd.

Germantown, MD 20876

301-972-3299 | www.butlersorchard.com

Approximately 45 minutes from downtown D.C.

Pick your own apples, pumpkins, or flowers at this family-friendly farm. Visit barnyard buddies too! The Strawberry Blossom Tour offered each spring is an educational group outing for children preschool through 3rd grade. Children experience a working farm; see how food is grown and harvested and enjoy a hands-on planting activity. Start a family tradition and choose and cut your own Christmas Tree from acres of carefully pruned Douglas Fir, Canaan Fir, and White Pine! The Holiday Open House includes a Hayride through the Christmas Trees, a marshmallow roast, and live music.

COLONIAL WILLIAMSBURG, VIRGINIA

www.history.org

Approximately two and a half hours from downtown D.C.

Colonial Williamsburg is the world's largest living-history museum. There are several buildings that remain on their 300 year-old-plus foundations! This recreated town is purely authentic. Superbly costumed interpreters tell the stories that transport you to the 18th century. "Revolutionary City" is especially family friendly and features a live dramatic program. It covers the period of 1774 to 1781 through a combination of large-scale streetscape events and multiple simultaneous vignettes. The street theater program makes you feel like you are actually part of Williamsburg during the years of the American Revolution. This performance will definitely capture the kids' attention spans (and educate them too!) Keep your eye on the website for the next new special event!

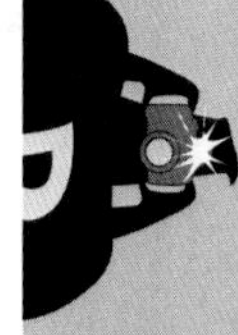

CLAUDE MOORE MEMORIAL FARM

310 Georgetown Pike
McLean, VA 22101
(703) 442-7557 | www.1771.org

Approximately 20 minutes from downtown D.C.

The year is 1771 here! Watch the family tend their farm and feel free to ask questions keeping with the spirit of recreating the past, you will be answered as if you were visiting in the 18th century. Visitors are also welcomed and encouraged to help the farm family with their chores including carding wool, mixing Johnnycake batter, weeding the garden and hoeing the fields. The family is grateful for all the help they can get! Younger children and toddlers will enjoy splashing in the washtub or watching the geese. Children of all ages and WonderDads will love visiting with the farm animals! Admission is $3 and $2 for children under 12.

CRUMLAND FARMS

7612 Willow Rd.
Frederick, MD 21702-2547
(301) 845-8099 | www.crumland.com

Approximately one hour and ten minutes from downtown D.C.

Crumland Farms hosts several family-friendly seasonal events throught out the year. The Annual Corn Festival features live music, "Bovine Bingo", moon bounce, and a Corn Maze! Pumpkin and apple picking are available throughout the fall. Hayrides can be arranged for groups of twenty or more. The spring features an Easter Egg Hunt and a "Pizza Farm" to teach kids where pizza ingredients come from. The Holiday Lights Spectacular each December is a must-see. The spectacular is a mile-long wonderland of dazzling light displays for young and old. Enjoy one delightful animated scene after another, including Rudolph's Flight School, Holiday at the Zoo, Victorian Holiday and Toy Land—all from the warmth and comfort of your own vehicle!

EASTERN SHORE, MARYLAND

Approximately one hour and ten minutes from downtown D.C.

Sit and relax and admire waterside sunsets or be adventurous and explore this serene peninsula. There are lighthouse tours, a wild life refuge, farms where you can pick your own fruit, and historic homes. The Marine Science Consortium is an excellent choice for families and offers many family workshops. The beaches, marshes, bays, maritime forests, and offshore waters of Virginia's Eastern Shore are The Consortium's classroom! Refuge Miniature Golf and Bumper Boats is another family must-do. The Pony Penning is a famous annual event each July in which "Salt Water Cowboys" herd the horses across the narrowest part of Assateague Channel at low tide.

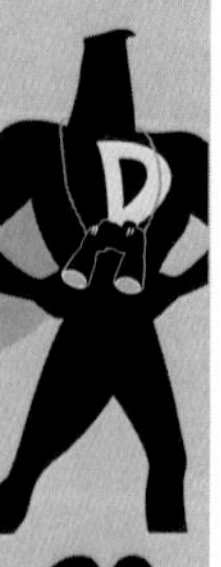

HARPER'S FERRY, WEST VIRGINIA

171 Shoreline Dr.
Harpers Ferry, WV 25425
www.nps.gov

Admission ranges from $4-$6.

Approximately one hour and twenty minutes from downtown D.C.

A visit to this quaint, historic community is like stepping into the past. Stroll the picturesque streets, visit exhibits and museums, or hike our trails and battlefields. There's a wide variety of experiences for visitors of all ages. Harpers Ferry National Historical park offers a wide choice of experiences for kids. From nature to history, from mountain hikes to river fishing, from ruined villages to quaint shops, from trains to canals, from battlefields to schoolyards, this town captures some of the coolest American stories ever told. Come churn butter, play lawn croquet, play a soldier, tend a garden, talk to a Union soldier or walk through silent ruins. Check the website for special scheduled events.

KINGS DOMINION

16000 Theme Park Way
Doswell, VA 23047
(804) 876-5000 | www.kingsdominion.com

General admission for a day starts at about $35 for those over three.

Approximately one hour and a half hours from downtown D.C.

The DC area's largest amusement park! One parent of small children waits in line, both ride with the park's innovative Parent Swap Pass! There is a lot to do here for little thrill-seekers. KidZville and Planet Snoopy are two of the dedicated children's areas featuring mini-sized rides and plenty of opportunities for a hug or photo op with a favorite Peanuts character. There is also a separate water park with wave pool, waterslides, kiddie pools, and a lazy river. Check the calander for special events and concerts.

LEESBURG ANIMAL PARK

19270 James Monroe Hwy.
Leesburg, VA
703 433 0002 | www.leesburganimalpark.com

Admission is $8 for children and $10 for adults

Approximately 50 minutes from downtown D.C.

The trip across the river is well worth it! Little ones can feed a baby bear from a bottle and hand feed other animals including llamas, nilgai antelope, deer, ducks, fish, and others. Meet other animals, domestic and exotic, up close! Kids can even ride a camel. There is also a fun playground and plenty of craft activities.

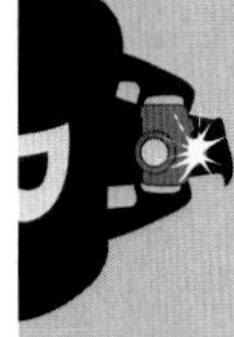

UNIQUE ADVENTURES

MANASSAS NATIONAL BATTLEFIELD

6511 Sudley Rd
Manassas, VA 20109-2358
(703) 361-1339 | www.nps.gov/mana

Approximately 30 minutes from downtown D.C.

There were two different battles fought at this park, which is also known as Bull Run. The best known was the first battle, which was the first major battle of the Civil War resulting in a defeat for the Union and the promotion of McClellan to head the Union army. Manassas national battlefield makes for an educational and economical afternoon for the whole family. The Civil War re-enactors often "recruit" the kids and have them join the army for the afternoon. The actors make it lots of fun and truly enjoy interacting with the children.

MONTICELLO

931 Thomas Jefferson Pkwy.
Charlottesville, VA 22902
9 am to 5 pm March through November; 10 am to 4 pm December through February
(434) 984-9822 | www.monticello.org

The family-friendly tour is free for children under 6, children 6-11 are $8, and adults are $22. Approximately two hours from downtown D.C.

Come see Thomas Jefferson's architectural masterpiece. The former president worked on the residence for over 40 years! Learn about life in the 18th century with hands-on activities like writing with a quill pen and playing 18th century games. You can also explore Jefferson's lifelong interest in gardening while enjoying the beauty and variety of Monticello's flower and vegetable gardens, grove, and orchards. The Griffin Discovery Room provides a variety of ways for little ones to connect with Thomas Jefferson, the members of the larger Monticello community, and learn about what life was like for children in the early 1800s. The space features reproduced elements from the Monticello house, such as Jefferson's alcove bed and Houdon's bust of Jefferson. Children and WonderDads can write on a polygraph machine, try on replicas of 18th-century clothes, learn how to weave, wield a facsimile blacksmith's hammer, touch a mastodon's jawbone, create secret codes on a wheel cipher based on Jefferson's design, play games popular in Jefferson's era, and engage in other self-directed activities.

MOUNT VERNON ESTATE

Historic Mount Vernon
3200 Mount Vernon Memorial Hwy.
Mount Vernon, VA 22309
(703) 780-2000 | www.mountvernon.org

For general passes, children 5 and under are free, children 6-11 are $7, and adults are $15. Approximately 30 minutes from downtown D.C.

The most scenic tourist attraction in Northern Virginia is the home of the "WonderDad" of our nation, George Washington. All kids are curious about this hero! Mount Vernon was originally an 8,000 acre mini-city divided into five farms. The farm where George Washington and his family lived was called the "Mansion House Farm." Today, this 500-acre farm is the part of the plantation that is open to visitors. There is plenty to see here in addition to the historic residence including stables, antique coaches, a blacksmith shop, a shoemaker, distillery, and even a dung repository! (Don't worry; it's no longer functioning) Check the website for fun family events!

NATIONAL WILDLIFE VISITOR'S CENTER

10901 Scarlet Tanager Ct.
Laurel, MD 20708-4011
(301) 497-5760 | www.fws.gov

Approximately 40 minutes from downtown D.C.

Perfect for the outdoorsy WonderDad! Discover the largest science and environmental education center in the entire Department of the Interior. Be a field researcher and travel through five life-scale habitat areas. Use the hands-on exhibits to learn about wildlife research, play I Spy in the amazing dioramas of gray wolves, whooping cranes, canvasback ducks and sea otters. Or take a half-hour guided tour through forest, meadows, and wetlands around the National Wildlife Visitor Center and let a ranger teach your kids (and you) all about this amazing resource. The tram is a 40 passenger, all-electric, open-air vehicle which provides a unique type of access to the wildlife and their habitats at the Patuxent Research Refuge. Hike one of the many trails or fish at Lake Allen, Cash Lake, or one of the many other bodies of water. Check the website for kid-geared workshops and programs!

NASA GODDARD VISITOR'S CENTER

800 Greenbelt Rd
Greenbelt, Md., 20771
www.nasa.gov

Approximately 25 minutes from downtown D.C.

The visitor center at NASA's Goddard Space Flight Center provides inspiration and a captivating educational experience for all ages. Visit the Goddard Rocket Gaden to see unique collection of space artifacts from the creation of NASA through today. There are interactive displays and models, as well as real examples of satellites and rocket flight hardware. They even have a piece of the moon! Admission is free.

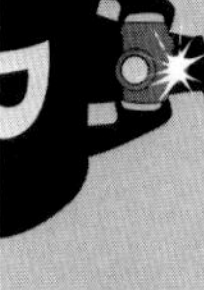

NATIONAL HARBOR, MARYLAND

www.nationalharbor.com

This spectacular waterfront community offers stunning views of downtown Washington, DC and Old Town Alexandria, and is just a 15-minute drive - or water taxi ride - to downtown D.C. The Washington Monuments boat cruise is the best way to see the D.C. sites. Canoe, kayak, and sailboat rentals are also available. There is always an exciting lineup of shows and events including circuses, plays, concerts and ice skating spectaculars. Future home of the National Children's museum.

OCEAN CITY, MARYLAND

Approximately three hours from downtown D.C.

The beach and the boardwalk are just the beginning! You'll find all kinds of kids' activities in Ocean City, Maryland. There are plenty of playgrounds, tot lots, tennis courts (including kid-size!), beach volleyball, softball, soccer and lacrosse fields, and more. Ocean City's extensive park system offers all kinds of opportunities for picnics, play and family fun. The Family Beach Olympics on the 27th Street beach. There are also free concerts, bonfires with story hours, and sundae Sundays in the park. Baja Amusements offers 10 acres of exciting family fun, featuring 8 go kart tracks, 2 climbing walls, bumper boats, kiddie rides, miniature golf, snack bar, arcade and much more. Pirate Adventures are swashbuckling fun for all. With painted faces and sailor sashes, the crew of determined little mates cast off on a childhood fantasy come true!

ZEKIAH FARMS

5235 Bryantown Rd.

Waldorf, Maryland 20601

240-216-4065 | www.zekiahfarms.com

Approximately 45 minutes from downtown D.C.

Get together with some other WonderDads and make a trip out to Zekiah Farms! Zekiah Farms offers a special itinerary for groups of children. Admission includes a corn maze, visits with the animals a make your own scarecrow (bring your own clothes!) a romp in the straw pit, face painting, and a pumpkin-picking. Zekiah Farms can also cater lunch upon request.

THE BEST DAD/CHILD SPORTING EVENTS

CHESAPEAKE BAYHAWKS

Navy-Marine Corps Memorial Stadium
550 Taylor Ave.
Annapolis, MD 21401
www.thebayhawks.com
May-August

Major League Lacrosse was founded in 2001 with the Bayhawks as one of the first six teams. Lacrosse is king here in the mid Atlantic and wildly popular with boys and girls alike. Any kid would love a trip to see the 2010 Steinfield-throphy winning Bayhawks.

DC UNITED

RFK Stadium
2400 E Capitol St. SE
Washington, DC 20003
www.dcunited.com
March-October

The WV Garage at RFK stadium is a great pre and during game hang out for kids. Try the Tigun Toss or Rabbit Kick, or just play some FIFA '10. Dads who own a Volkswagen get a free swag bag!

WASHINGTON CAPITALS

Verizon Center
601 F St. NW
Washington, DC 20004
(202) 628-3200 | www.capitals.nhl.com

Taking the kids to "rock the red" is a great idea. Washington's NHL team plays at the Verizon Center and there are plenty of kid-friendly restaurants and activities in Chinatown and nearby Penn Quarter. Mites on Ice and Kids on Ice are great kids programs offered by the team. Stop by Kettler Iceplex one day to watch practice the Caps practice too!

WASHINGTON GENERALS

www.washingtongenerals.com

The archrival of the Harlem Globetrotters! The General recently returned to D.C. in 2007. Catch this exhibition basketball team on a tour-stop in their home city.

WASHINGTON KASTLES

11th and H St. NW
Washington, DC 20005
www.washingtonkastles.com
Each July

Featuring stars such as the Williams sisters, the Kastles are the newest addition to the World Tennis Team professional tennis league. Each match consists of five sets of a different type of tennis (men's singles, men's doubles, women's singles, women's doubles, and mixed doubles) to keep it interesting. See professional tennis up close and personal in the heart of the city.

WASHINGTON MYSTICS

Verizon Center
601 F St. NW
Washington, DC 20004
(202) 628-3200 | www.wnba.com/mystics
May-August

One of the first WNBA teams to be established! The Mystics lead the WNBA in home-game attendance. Washington's WNBA team also sponsor a youth summer basketball league for girls ten and up.

WASHINGTON NATIONALS

2201 S Capitol St. SE
Washington, DC 20002
www.washington.nationals.mlb.com
March-October

There isn't a more classic dad and kid outing than a day at the ballpark! The Nationals have a brand new stadium and play right in D.C. Tours of the ballpark are also available.

WASHINGTON REDSKINS

FedEx Field
1600 FedEx Way
Landover, MD 20785
www.redskins.com
August-January

D.C.'s NFL football team hosts a Redskins Kids Club featuring special events such as movie nights at FedEx field , training camp visits, a mini combine and contests.

WASHINGTON REDSKINS CHEERLEADERS

More than 200 young girls ages five and up enroll in the Junior Redskins Cheerleader Program. The program is designed to teach girls fundamentals of dance, showmanship and performance. Enrollment is open to the first 200 girls to sign up. One of the first NFL cheerleading teams, the Redskins Cheerleaders make over 300 appearances in the area a year—check the website to see when they'll be performing in a neighborhood near you.

WASHINGTON WIZARDS

Verizon Center
601 F St. NW
Washington, DC 20004
(202) 628-3200 | www.nba.com/wizards
October-April

The Wizards also play in the Verizon Center. The NBA team also sponsors several family-friendly pre-game events. "Fan Fests" feature face painters, balloon artists, skills and drills demos and much more.

THE WIZARDS GIRLS

The Wizards Girls often offer special behind-the-scenes backstage passes. Check the website for more information.

BOWIE BAYSOX

Prince George's Stadium
4101 Crain Hwy.
Bowie, MD 20716
www.baysox.com
April-September

Louie, the lovable Baysox mascot has a special kids club featuring several fun events throughout the season.

FREDERICK KEYS

Harry Grove Stadium
21 Stadium Drive
Frederick, MD 21701
web.minorleaguebaseball.com
April-September

Membership in the Junior Keys is free and includes free tickets, ice cream sundaes, pizza, and other free treats on select game nights. Kids can also celebrate their birthdays with the Keys!

POTOMAC NATIONALS

G. Richard Pfitzner Stadium
7 County Complex Court
Woodbridge, VA 22192
web.minorleaguebaseball.com
April-September

Kids Club members get loads of perks, including a grandstand ticket to every Sunday home game, and an invitation to the Meet the Players Picnic, their own personalized membership card and much more!

WASHINGTON CRICKET LEAGUE

www.wclinc.com
April-November

Shake things up! There are over 25 cricket teams in the DC metro area. Teams play throughout Maryland, Virgina, and D.C.

WASHINGTON IRISH RUGBY CLUB

East Potomac Park
Washington, DC 20024
www.washingtonirishfc.com
August-November

Show the kids a new sport! The team practices at 5th and P St. NW at Bundy Field on Tuesdays and Thursdays at 6:30 pm.

AMERICAN UNIVERSITY EAGLES

Bender Arena
4400 Massachusetts Ave. NW
Washington, DC 20016
(202) 885-3267 | www.aueagles.com

The field hockey team has been Patriot League champions for seven years. The men's basketball team also excels. These student athletes make great role models—the athletic department has been honored several times for having a high percentage of students on the Dean's List. Bender arena is home to the basketball, volleyball, and wrestling teams.

GEORGETOWN UNIVERSITY HOYAS

McDonough Arena
3700 O St. NW
Washington, DC 20057
(202) 687-HOYA or (202) 687-2449 | www.guhoyas.com

What's a Hoya? Go to a game and find out! Men's basketball games at the Verizon Center are the most popular. Most other sports are played at McDonough Arena. Check the website for more events!

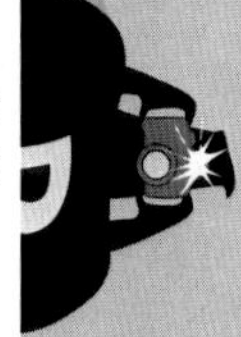

GEORGE MASON UNIVERSITY PATRIOTS

703-993-3270 | www.gomason.cstv.com

$30 gets you all-access to all fall sports (and a cool scarf). George Mason is accessible by metro on the orange line.

GEORGE WASHINGTON UNIVERSITY COLONIALS

The Smith Center
600 22nd St. NW
Washington, DC 20052
(202) 994-6050 | www.gwsports.com

The Colonials have most of their games and matches right in downtown DC at the Smith Center. Hail to the Buff and Blue!

HOWARD UNIVERSITY BISON

Cramton Auditorium
2455 Sixth St. NW
Washington, DC 20059
202-806-7198/7189 | www.howard-bison.com

Catch a football game and see Howard's famous and award-winning marching band, the Marching Bison. Women's tennis has been on fire recently.

THE UNIVERSITY OF MARYLAND TERRAPINS (TERPS)

Byrd Stadium (football and men's lacrosse)
Comcast Center (basketball, volleyball wrestling)
301-314-7070 or 800-IM-A-TERP | www.umterps.com

Basketball and lacrosse rule at University of Maryland College Park. (Oh and a "terrapin" is a turtle of some kind).

AT&T NATIONAL GOLF TOURNAMENT

8500 River Rd.
Bethesda, MD 20817
www.attnational.org

The Tiger Woods' Foundation AT & T National Golf Tour will soon be returning to DC in 2012 after two years in Philadelphia. 120 top PGA Tour golfers compete over the course of the week. Children under 12 are free!

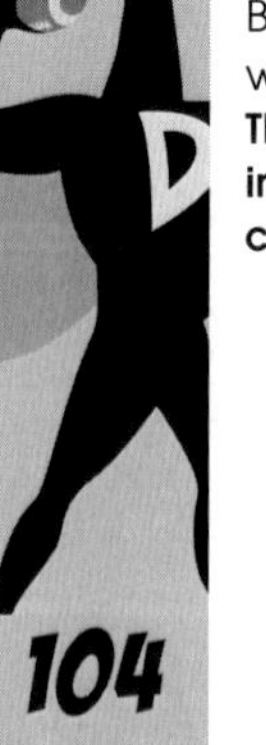

DRAGON BOAT FESTIVAL

Thompson's Boat Center
2900 Virginia Ave. NW
Washington DC
www.dragonboatdc.com

The Washington DC Dragon Boat Festival is an annual event held each May. The two-day festival features competitive dragon boat races on the Potomac River, colorful cultural performances and hands-on activities. Approximately 60 teams from all over the east coast compete in these thrilling races. Kids will love the crazy-looking boats.

LEGG MASON TENNIS CLASSIC

William H.G. Fitzgerald Tennis Center
16th & Kennedy Sts. NW
Washington, DC 20011
www.leggmasontennisclassic.com

The Legg Mason Tennis Classic is hosted in DC each summer and is one of the Top 20 Men's Tennis Tournaments in the world. Held in beautiful Rock Creek Park, there is plenty to do and see after the tournament.

WASHINGTON INTERNATIONAL HORSE SHOW

Verizon Center
601 F St. NW
Washington, DC 20004
(202) 628-3200 | www.wihs.org

Held each fall, this event is free for kids (and only $10 for parents). There are plenty of fun events to watch throughout the weekend, however, each year the festival has a dedicated "Kids Day" offering free pony rides, a horse grooming station, a chance to meet Bubbles, a miniature horse, a book nook and arts and crafts.

ABOUT THE AUTHOR

Caroline became immediately active in Washington D.C. upon moving to the city in 2008. She participates in local civic and philanthropic activities, managed a successful spa at a top hotel, and gained familiarity with family-friendly D.C. locales through extensive research, personal visits and with the invaluable help of the the local parenting community. She is currently completing graduate work on her masters in writing at Georgetown University.

THANK YOUS

Caroline would like to thank the many people who contributed to making this project a success. She would particularly like to thank her family—Courtney, Jim, Billy, Mom and Dad; her friends—Katherine, Molly, Mary, Dave, and John; and the amazing DC WonderDads—Mike Long, Vincent diCaro, Roland Warren, and John Taylor, for their support.